PA RIS

T0307082

Travel with Marco Polo
Insider Tips

MARCO POLO
TOP HIGHLIGHTS

MUSÉE DU LOUVRE ⭐
You could spend weeks exploring and marvelling in the world's most extensive museum.

📷 *Tip: Yes, the glass pyramid outside is great for a photo, but so is the inverted pyramid in the Carrousel du Louvre.*

➤ p. 33

EIFFEL TOWER (TOUR EIFFEL) ⭐
Have you even been to Paris if you haven't seen it?

📷 *Tip: The Iron Lady is best viewed from the Trocadero on the other side of the Seine.*

➤ p. 44

MUSÉE D'ORSAY ⭐
The Impressionists are sure to impress in this museum, housed in a glamorous Belle-Époque former railway station.

📷 *Tip: Capture the Paris cityscape from the two giant clocks.*

➤ p. 46

ARC DE TRIOMPHE ⭐
The city's second landmark is a great spot to gaze out over the Champs-Élysées and 11 other avenues.

📷 *Tip: Before you head back down, snap a picture of the view from the stairs.*

➤ p. 48

PLACE DES VOSGES ⭐
This charming old royal square is at the heart of the lively Marais quarter.

➤ p. 37

ÎLE DE LA CITÉ 🖲
Like the neighbouring Île Saint-Louis, this island in the Seine, full of chic shops and cafés, is the perfect spot for a stroll.

➤ p. 30

JARDIN DU LUXEMBOURG 🄵
The subject of many a song, this park in the heart of the city is a good choice for a relaxing walk.

➤ p. 44

NOTRE-DAME 🄸
A fire seriously damaged the world-famous cathedral in spring 2019, but President Emmanuel Macron is determined to restore it to its former glory by 2024.

➤ p. 39

VERSAILLES 🄹
A visit to the home of the Sun King is a must. Just half an hour from Paris, the vast palace is surrounded by a magnificent park, where you can picnic, cycle and row (photo).

➤ p. 68

MONTMARTRE 🄺
Known for its artists, this hill – with its domed Sacré-Cœur basilica – crowns the metropolis.
📷 *Tip: For a great view of the hill and basilica, head to the Centre Pompidou in the city centre.*

➤ p. 61, p. 135

CONTENTS

🕐	Plan your visit	☂	Rainy day activities
€–€€€	Price ranges	🐷	Budget activities
(*)	Premium-rate telephone number	🃏	Family activities
		🚩	Classic experiences

(𝄘 A2) Removable pull-out map
(0) Address located off the pull-out map

CONTENTS

BEST OF
PARIS

The Eiffel Tower: 10,100 tonnes of ironwork

BEST ☂

WHEN IT RAINS

ACTIVITIES TO BRIGHTEN YOUR DAY

SHOPPING OUT OF THE RAIN

Paris has numerous department stores and covered passages that are ideal for souvenir-hunting during a downpour. The *Carrousel du Louvre* shopping centre is architecturally stunning and its shops are open on Sundays.

➤ p. 34

MUSEUM OF FOREIGN CULTURES

Already ticked off all the "must-sees" from your list of museums? If these didn't include the impressive *Musée du Quai Branly – Jacques Chirac*, you can easily while away a few hours here.

➤ p. 45

GO UNDERGROUND

Paris has an extensive underground world. As well as the Métro and sewage systems, the city is also home to the *catacombs*, a system of tunnels over 300km long, holding the remains of more than six million people.

➤ p. 56

DINE LIKE AN ARISTOCRAT (OR JUST TAKE A LOOK)

While away the time until the sun reappears in the midst of gilded grandeur at the most beautiful railway station restaurant in the world, *Le Train Bleu* (photo). You don't even need to have a meal here to experience its majesty – just enjoy the sumptuousness of the comfortable leather chairs.

➤ p. 79

FOR BOOKWORMS & NIGHT OWLS

You'll need plenty of time to shop for music, books and films at the city's top venue, *Fnac*. It's located on the Champs-Elysées and stays open until after 10pm.

➤ p. 92

BEST 🐷
ON A BUDGET

FOR SMALLER WALLETS

ORGAN CONCERTS
A number of churches regularly offer free concerts. The rich sound of organ music resonating through the church of *Saint Eustache* next to the Forum des Halles is more than impressive – both visually and acoustically.
➤ p. 40

BEAUTIFUL VIEWS – FOR FREE
For an alternative view over Paris to the Eiffel Tower or the Arc de Triomphe, head to the roof of the *Institut du Monde Arabe* or visit the roof terrace of the *Galeries Lafayette* on Boulevard Haussmann.
➤ p. 41, p. 97

FREE MUSEUM ADMISSION
Many museums in Paris do not charge admission; one of the most highly recommended is the *Musée d'Art Moderne de la Ville de Paris*.
➤ p. 59

IT'S GOOD TO BE YOUNG
Cultural events and institutions are often free for young people – why spend money on theatre tickets when they can attend performances like the ones at the *Comédie Française* for free on certain days?
➤ p. 115

SKATERS' PARADISE
Keen to discover Paris on wheels but worried about the traffic? We've got you! Every Friday evening, nearly 20 miles of the city are closed off for rollerbladers. The fun begins at 10pm at Montparnasse station (photo).
➤ p. 118

BEST

WITH CHILDREN

FUN FOR YOUNG & OLD

VERY MUCH ALIVE OR STUFFED AND BONY
The *Natural History Museum* is located in the *Jardin des Plantes*, which is also home to a horticultural teaching garden. There's a zoo here, too, and that's the real hit when the weather is good. But if it's still raining, choose between the garden's greenhouses, the evolution gallery and dinosaur bones.
➤ p. 43

SHIP AHOY!
Much of childhood in Paris plays out in the city's parks and green spaces. After all, there are climbing frames, merry-go-rounds, pony rides and, in some parks, even miniature sailing boats for kids to sail on ponds. One of the most famous spots for sailing fun is the *Jardin du Luxembourg*.
➤ p. 44

MICKEY VS ASTERIX
You can choose between several amusement parks in Paris and the surrounding area. You just have to decide whether you want to go to *Disneyland* (photo), *Parc Astérix* or the *Jardin d'Acclimatation*.
➤ p. 60, p. 65

CANAL CRUISE WITH A SPECIAL ENDING
Take a boat trip along the Seine, via the Canal Saint-Martin and the Canal de l'Ourcq, to the *Parc de la Villette*, where you will find themed gardens, adventure playgrounds, a 360-degree big screen and the *Cité des Sciences et de l'Industrie* science museum.
➤ p. 64

CIRQUE D'HIVER
Inaugurated in 1852 by Napoleon, the *Cirque d'Hiver*, or Winter Circus, is a true Parisian institution.
➤ p. 115

ARCADES – NOSTALGIE À LA FRANÇAISE

Paris is defined by the splendour of its past. Upscale covered shopping centres, such as the *Galerie Vivienne* (photo), have existed since the 18th century and are typical of parts of the city, even today.
➤ p. 36

MUSEUMS OF INTERNATIONAL RENOWN

Alongside the *Louvre* – the museum with the largest exhibition space in the world – the *Centre Pompidou* boasts the largest collection of modern art in Europe today. The museum that best reflects Paris, however, is the *Musée d'Orsay*, with its collection of works by the French Impressionists.
➤ p. 46

GOURMET MECCA

Nowhere else in the world have so many stars graced both chefs and restaurants as in Paris. Yet traditional bistros and brasseries such as *Bofinger* are still the gastronomic heart of the city, offering the best quality food and an amazing ambiance.
➤ p. 74

LUXURIOUS SHOPPING

Paris, as the epitome of luxury, is celebrated for its champagne, perfume and fashion. You can shop a large selection of luxury items in the "*Triangle d'Or*" – the golden triangle around the *rue du Faubourg Saint-Honoré*.
➤ p. 97

INNER-CITY MARKET WITH MULTICULTURAL FLAIR

Chinese people, Indians and North Africans have all brought their cultures to Paris and injected a multicultural flair into different districts of the city. The bustling *Marché Barbès* is a tantalising example.
➤ p. 101

GET TO KNOW PARIS

The opulent Fontaine des Mers on the Place de la Concorde

DISCOVER PARIS

The cafés and street artists create a village-like atmosphere on the Place du Tertre

Paris has always been a metropolis where only the best is good enough, a city of superlatives: faster, prettier, bigger, glossier than most other cities. All it takes is a stroll along the magnificent mile-long Champs-Elysées – particularly when illuminated by hundreds of thousands of lights on a December evening – or a coffee at a street café as you watch the hustle and bustle of the vibrant Saint-Germain-des-Prés district with its student life and many nightclubs, to be infected by the charm of this city.

LEFT AND RIGHT OF THE SEINE

At 105.4sq km, Paris is less than a tenth of the geographical size of Greater London, making it a highly walkable or bikeable city. Paris consists of 20 districts, known as *arrondissements*, that expand out in a spiral from the 1st

3rd century BC
The Parisii settle on the Île de la Cité

360
Lutetia is renamed Paris

1257
Sorbonne University is founded

1345
Notre-Dame cathedral is finally finished after a good 180 years of building work

1789
The storming of the Bastille on 14 July marks the start of the French Revolution

1871
Proclamation of the German Empire in Versailles

arrondissement at the heart of the city. Parisians associate very specific clichés with each arrondissement number. The 16th arrondissement, for example, is synonymous with the bourgeoisie, while the 11th is coolness personified. Conveniently, street signs always also indicate which arrondissement you're currently located in. You'll start to spot the clichés that characterise the individual arrondissements yourself pretty quickly.

The Seine divides the city into *rive gauche* in the south and *rive droite* in the north. There's also a societal dividing line between the well-to-do districts in the west and the poorer quarters in the east of the city.

A BIRD'S EYE VIEW

You can get a good overview of the city from the observation platform on the sixth floor of the Centre Georges Pompidou, which lies right in the city centre. From here, Paris spreads out like an open book beneath you. The bright mobile sculptures and cascading water of the Stravinsky Fountain lie at your feet and, further up, the towers of famous Notre-Dame Cathedral loom into view. It stands on the Île de la Cité, the actual nucleus of the city, where the Parisii settled in the third century BC. A bit further afield, you'll recognise the towers of the former prison, la Conciergerie. Even further away and slightly to the right, you can see the sprawling giant complex of the Louvre, a former royal palace that now houses the largest museum in the world.

To the right, behind you, is the sparkling golden dome of Les Invalides,

1889
The Eiffel Tower is built for the *Exposition Universelle*

1940–44
German occupation in World War II

2015
A number of terrorist attacks shake the city

2016
Together with 130 suburban communes, Paris becomes the "Métropole du Grand Paris"

2019
Notre-Dame goes up in flames. Reconstruction completion date set for 2024

2024
Paris hosts the summer Olympics for the third time

Napoleon's final resting place. Not far away, the symbol of the city, the Eiffel Tower, looms on the horizon. To the far right and to the west, you can pick out the high-rises in La Défense, Europe's largest office district. Look further to the right and north, and you'll see the dazzling white church, Sacré-Cœur, which crowns the highest peak of the former artists' hill, Montmartre.

THE HEART OF CENTRALISM

Paris has been the vibrant political, economic and cultural epicentre of France for centuries. As the residence of kings and the seat of government, and by virtue of its numerous universities, Paris was also recognised as an intellectual centre in Europe as far back as the Middle Ages. It has been the workplace for countless artists, writers and architects, and a continual source of unrest and uprisings. Paris was the stage for many revolutions. The great revolution of 1789, known for its motto "liberty, equality, fraternity", even became a symbol for the fight against oppression, although the rights championed mostly benefited the bourgeoisie and not the lower classes. Strikes and demonstrations still frequently occur in Paris, and every French government fears mobilisation in the streets, with pension reform being one of the most recent bones of contention. Riots also broke out in 2023 following the shooting of a teenager by police.

FROM CHIC TO STREET ART

What gives Paris its special flair? For some, it's the grand boulevards, so ideal for strolling. For others, it's the lure of luxury boutiques on the rue du Faubourg Saint-Honoré or shopping in world-renowned department stores such as Galeries Lafayette or Printemps, famed for their extravagant Christmas decorations. Others are content to explore the incredible variety of museums of international renown, to stroll along the Seine, sit in a street café or relax in one of the many parks, picnic along the Canal Saint-Martin – or just go with the flow. Even the older, provincial-style, unvarnished Paris still exists: attractive alleyways, crooked little buildings housing cafés or pleasant restaurants, and shops with enticing displays and chattering shopkeepers. There is a hubbub of activity around the fascinating markets, with their colourful displays of fruit and vegetables, all kinds of cheese, sausages and meat, plus fish and seafood, pastries and cakes, and vendors who loudly tout their wares.

This folksy side of Paris is typical of the north and east of the city, for example in Belleville, which is inhabited by a large number of immigrants, but also artists and young families, since living costs are still affordable here. Here, you can experience art for free in an outdoor setting: rue Denoyez is the spot for graffiti and street artists, who bring some colour to the grey tones of this working-class neighbourhood. Hidden behind modern residential blocks, winding alleys like Villa de l'Ermitage and Cité Leroy – with their tiny houses – give us a glimpse of how the area must have looked in the 19th century. The hilltop neighbourhood

Graffiti on the rue Denoyez in Belleville

of Butte aux Cailles has also maintained some of its old-world charm; its bistros and affordable restaurants attract a younger Parisian crowd.

ONCE AN ARTISTS' METROPOLIS

It is no coincidence that major art movements such as Impressionism and Cubism found their beginnings here. Painters like Auguste Renoir, Vincent van Gogh and Pablo Picasso, as well as writers such as Voltaire, Victor Hugo, Honoré de Balzac, Charles Baudelaire, Marcel Proust, Ernest Hemingway and Jean-Paul Sartre, lived and worked here. Artists met in cafés and brasseries that have since become famous on the left bank of the Seine – the *rive gauche*. This area, around the university buildings of the Sorbonne, has long been the intellectual heart of the city. The majority of these meeting places, such as Café de Flore, or the existentialists' rendezvous Les Deux Magots in Saint-Germain-des-Prés, or the Closerie des Lilas in the former artists' district of Montparnasse, still exist today. These cafés and restaurants are a welcome place to stop by, especially for tourists and the well-heeled. But they, like the rest of the affluent metropolis, have long since become too expensive for poor poets and struggling artists.

MULTICULTURAL

Paris has always been home to a diverse mixture of people from various backgrounds. Centuries ago, it was the Bretons, Auvergneses, Alsatians and Basques who came to Paris in search of a better life and enriched the city – it was the Alsatians who first introduced their brasseries. Much later, people arrived from former French colonies in Africa – today there is a wonderfully colourful African market in Goutte d'Or every Sunday – and the Chinese – who settled in Place d'Italie where they opened markets, businesses and restaurants. While, in the past, the city opened its arms to the politically persecuted, as well as revolutionaries such as Karl Marx and Leon Trotsky, and granted asylum to refugees from Nazi Germany, today the city shows a different face. Since the start of the refugee crisis in 2015, thousands of migrants have been left living in appalling conditions on the streets or in makeshift, improvised tent camps in Paris and its surrounding suburbs.

UNAFFORDABLE

Home to all classes of society for centuries, Paris is now increasingly becoming a capital for the rich. A cappuccino can easily cost more than 5 euros, an evening meal served with wine, 60 euros or more. A statutory cap on rents is intended, at the very least, to make housing more affordable. However, the law does nothing to improve the poor condition of many residential buildings. The extravagantly ornate palace façades often conceal shabby backstairs and cramped attic rooms. These *chambres des bonnes*, the former servants' quarters, are now rented out to students and the less well off. In an effort to improve the housing situation and avoid further ghettoisation, the city is now purchasing real estate in upscale districts in the city centre in order to renovate them and convert them into subsidised housing.

GRAND PARIS

Today, several ambitious projects are in the works, intended to make the city more liveable. The latest major project is entitled Le Grand Paris. The city of museums had grown too cramped and decided to open its arms to the surrounding suburbs, which were incorporated into the city. Paris is now building on what Napoleon III began in 1860, with the incorporation of Montmartre, Belleville and nine other communities. In January 2016, Paris and 130 neighbouring communities merged to form the Métropole du Grand Paris, which is home to more than seven million people. Important infrastructure packages have been passed in an effort to improve transport links and mitigate the chaotic traffic that often throttles the city streets. By 2030, four additional Métro lines are set to be added to the existing 14 to connect Paris to the surrounding communities. There is currently a flurry of construction activity in the high-rise district of La Défense, and skyscrapers are also going up along the city's inner ring road – much to the dismay of many Parisians. The city's stated goal is to defend its rank as a global capital against megacities like London, Tokyo, and New York.

AT A GLANCE

2.2 MILLION
inhabitants "intra muros" (within the Paris administrative district) 7 million in "Le Grand Paris"
Greater London: 9,648,000

10
Michelin 3-star restaurants

London: 5

674
steps to the second floor of the Eiffel Tower: 1,665 to the top
St Paul's Cathedral dome, London: 528 steps

105km^2
Area "intra muros"

Berlin: 1,569km^2

LONGEST STREET: RUE DE VAUGIRARD

4,360m
Shortest street: rue Degrès at 5.75m

MONA LISA

15,000
PEOPLE ADMIRE THE PICTURE EVERY DAY AT THE LOUVRE

GARE DU NORD

207 million
PASSENGERS USE THE STATION EACH YEAR

2 UNESCO WORLD HERITAGE SITES

The banks of the Seine between Pont de Sully and Pont d'Iéna, and Versailles

1,119
people were beheaded at Place de la Concorde during the French Revolution

OLDEST TREE
A black locust tree planted in 1601 in Square René Viviani

90,000 PIGEONS LIVE IN PARIS
LONDON: NEARLY 3 MILLION

UNDERSTAND PARIS

PARIS 2024

After three rejections from the International Olympic Committee, Paris is now on cloud 2024, not nine! Exactly 100 years since the city last hosted the Olympics, the Summer Games will once again be held on the Seine. Since the announcement was made, building after building site has appeared, despite the fact that 95 per cent of the necessary infrastructure was already in place. The city was determined to use this opportunity to give itself a makeover. Projects include the renovation of the Grand Palais, a magnificent 1900 building that hosts exhibitions and sports events, and the removal of the toxic asbestos that coats the Tour Montparnasse.

The hope is that the Olympics will motivate Parisians to get more active, with the goal of having a sports ground within a five-minute radius of every Parisian. But how is this going to work? Simple – by setting up free public exercise equipment all over the city! The longest fitness course, at 5km, is between Métro Nation in the 12th and Métro Stalingrad in the 10th arrondissement. The excuse that it's too expensive to join the gym won't fly in this Olympic city!

ON SET IN PARIS

Paris and the cinema have a long shared history. It all started in 1895 with the first public film screening by the Lumière brothers. Since then, Paris has been immortalised in countless films. Around 900 film shoots take place in the city every year. You've probably heard of films like *Amélie*, Woody Allen's *Midnight in Paris* and *Untouchable*. If you're interested in retracing the footsteps of film history in the city, contact Juliette Dubois from *Ciné-Balade (cine-balade.com)*. This cinema expert can regale you with countless anecdotes – in English – about the world of cinema in Paris. If you want to explore on your own, a collection of locations that have made their mark on film history is available on *parisfaitsoncinema.com*.

THIRSTY?

Many things are more expensive in Paris than they are elsewhere. But there's one thing you can have as much of as you want for free: high-quality tap water. As well as it being completely normal to order a carafe of tap water *(carafe d'eau)* with your meal, you'll also find public drinking fountains in many places. The most famous of these is the *Fontaine Wallace*: the Four Graces from Roman mythology carry a dome decorated with dolphins. And yes: You can actually drink the water flowing through the middle. Why "Wallace"? Because after the Franco-Prussian War in 1872, the fountains were commissioned and donated to the city by an Englishman named Richard Wallace. Today, more than 100 of these green, cast-iron, Renaissance-style fountains are still in operation throughout Paris.

Café des Deux Moulins was a filming location for *Le Fabuleux Destin d'Amélie Poulain* – better known *as Amélie* in English

In parks and outside public toilets, too, you will find taps providing potable water. Recently, drinking fountains that produce carbonated water *(eau pétillante)* have been added around town. Yes, you read that right: 🐷 free sparkling water for everyone! You can find the addresses of all the drinking fountains on *eaudeparis.fr/carte-des-fontaines*.

SIDER TIP
Sparkling fountains

ORGANICALLY BEAUTIFUL

France has long lagged behind other countries in terms of environmental awareness. Now, it's playing catch-up. Paris is in the grips of organic fever – the supermarket chain *bio c' bon* *(bio-c-bon.eu)* alone has opened more than 50 branches in the French capital over the last few years. The city's northeast is known as the home of the "Bourgeois-Bohème" (Bobo for short), who live with their families in former factories converted into loft apartments, and their younger brothers, the hipsters, who zip through the city on their fixie bikes. A new organic venue opens here nearly every week. For everything from cosmetics *(mademoiselle-bio.com)* and fashion *(ekyog.com)* to fast food *(bioburger.fr)*, customers' main concern today is that it's organic. You can find hundreds of listings for Paris's burgeoning organic scene on the website *Paris so Biotiful – le green city Guide (parisobiotiful. com)*.

MÉTRO STATIONS

Paris has had an underground railway system since 1900, and, with more than 300 stations, it is one of the most densely knit networks in the world. There is supposedly no station in Paris further than 500m from the next, and Paris would not be Paris without the famous wrought-iron Art Nouveau Métro entrances by the artist Hector Guimard (1867–1942).

The arabesque-shaped *bouche du metro* (mouth of the Métro) at the station *Porte Dauphine* is particularly eye-catching, with its flowers in the form of red lamps that grow out of the vine-like ironwork. The modern counterpart to the some 80 Guimard entrances still in use is the glass masterpiece *Kiosque des Noctambules* (Night Owls' Pavilion), created by Jean-Michel Othoniel. With its colourful glass spheres, it graces the entrance to the station *Palais Royal-Musée de Louvre* on the square in front of La Comédie Française. Tastefully illuminated statues point the way to the largest museum in the world at the *Louvre* underground station. Also worth a look is the *Arts et Metier* station, clad entirely in copper with huge cogwheels echoing the days of steam engines; it is considered one of the most beautiful in the city. A wall mural at the *Bastille* station commemorates the mercurial history of the site, while the *Cluny-Sorbonne* station has been embellished with beautiful mosaics by Jean René Bazaine, and its ceiling bears the names of famous former students of the nearby university.

The Art Nouveau entrance to Saint Michel métro station

PARIS WITHOUT A CAR

Paris is choked to death by traffic. The Boulevard Périphérique is not the only ring road notorious for traffic jams. Inner city roads are also susceptible to gridlocks. Whenever the hot-air balloon over the Parc Citroën changes its colour to red, the air in the metropolis has become so dirty that it can be a danger to health. It is therefore no surprise that the mayor, Anne Hidalgo, wants to ban cars from the city centre as much as possible.

Step by step, the central districts are set to become strictly controlled traffic areas, and vehicles with combustion engines are to be banned completely by 2030.

Certain streets and districts are closed to car traffic on Sundays, which helps reduce air pollution. This includes the Marais, the waterfront streets of the Canal Saint-Martin and the Champs-Élysées (one Sunday a month). The city even introduced one completely car-free day per year (parissansvoiture.fr). A 2.3-km stretch along the left bank of the Seine, between the Musée du Quai Branly and the Musée d'Orsay, has banned cars entirely. Today, it is lined with floating gardens, bars, restaurants, sports equipment and activities for kids and grownups alike. The closure of a further section of roads between the Pont Neuf and the Bassin de l'Arsenal has caused jubilation among nearby residents and grumbling among motorists.

A viable alternative to a car is the bike rental system or e-scooters (see p. 149).

TRUE OR FALSE?

CITY OF LOVE... YEAH, RIGHT!

Couples from all over the world flock to Paris to celebrate their love. But what they don't realise is that the beauty of the Seine can have a rather toxic effect on relationships. Word of this danger has spread among Parisians, with many leaving Paris in a hurry once they find their life partner. Safely tucked far away from temptation in their detached houses, they hope to escape the city's vast divorce rate.

PARK COMME FONT LES FRANÇAIS

Have you ever tried parking like the French? In Paris, the usual technique is an inch here, an inch there, forwards, backwards... Bumper to bumper, Parisians skilfully manoeuvre their car until it is squeezed into an impossibly small space.

STRIKE = NO CHAOS

Yes, the French do like to strike. But don't go thinking that travel strikes mean Paris is regularly in chaos. It's only foreign camera teams that go out in search of citizens desperately trying to reach their workplace. Parisians have long since preferred to spend their strikes differently, whether that's working from home, having a day off or cycling to the office.

A taste of Africa in the 18th arrondissement: fishmongers at the Marché du Château Rouge

PARIS IS STILL A FEAST

Paris is known for its packed cafés, restaurants and concert halls. After the terrorist attacks of November 2015, you might have thought those places would have been abandoned – but quite the opposite happened. With grim determination, many Parisians returned to the terraces of their favourite cafés within days after the attacks. And in a show of solidarity, visiting globetrotters joined them. Enjoying a meal or a glass of wine outdoors became a statement, an affirmation of the values of the French Republic: liberty, equality and fraternity. Then UN Secretary General Ban Ki-moon himself stopped by to have a cup of coffee with the mayor of Paris. And it didn't take long before crowds were rocking out at the *Le Bataclan* concert hall (see p. 111) again.

Today, strict security measures remain in place. Originally created in 1978, "Plan Vigipirate" is France's national security alert system. In concrete terms today, it means bag searches and a heightened police and security presence in some museums, bars and clubs. Visiting some clubs is like going through airport security – you're searched before you can enter, and you have to empty your water bottle. Bear in mind that in France you must be able to prove your identity, either by providing documents when asked or within four hours at a police station.

BERLIN BUZZ

Frederick the Great once said that he would never have the foolish arrogance to presume Berlin could one day compare to Paris. Well, today many young Parisians think differently and are pushing back against the historical weightiness of their city. They come back from Berlin buzzing with ideas and try to breathe some of the German capital's creative spark into Paris. *Berlinons Paris* (Let's Berlin Paris) is the name of a collective determined to promote electronic music and urban art. Its members spontaneously occupy abandoned industrial sites before new building begins; the media hypes these new creative spaces as hip locations *á la berlinoise*. Even without much publicity, word of a new hotspot spreads like wildfire on social networks. So, rather than hopping on the next plane to Berlin, Paris's cool crowd has started meeting at run-down freight yards with graffiti and food trucks.

PARIS INTERNATIONAL

Couldn't afford the cost of a trip around the world, so you opted for a city break in Paris instead? Not a bad choice – after all, you can experience the entire world here, condensed into about 100 sqkm. If Parisians want to experience India, they head to *Passage Brady*, where they'll find row upon row of Indian restaurants. Here and on rue du Faubourg Saint-Denis between Gare du Nord and La Chapelle, you'll find every souvenir you could have possibly brought back from a trip to India. *Rue Saint-Anne* may still be named after a French queen, but it has been firmly under Japanese control for years. *Chinatown*, on the other hand, is located in the 13th arrondissement, and if you exit the Métro at *Château Rouge*, you'll find yourself in the midst of a colourful, bustling African street market.

PICNIC

Parisians enjoy sitting outdoors. And in the light of increasingly high costs, many residents and tourists have discovered the simple pleasure of a picnic at the appearance of the first rays of spring sunshine. A favourite spot is the pedestrian bridge, *Pont des Arts*, which has a view towards the Louvre and Île de la Cité – on warm evenings, there is rarely enough space here. The same goes for the parks around the Eiffel Tower.

The sunlit quays along the Seine are even more popular, especially in the afternoon. There's a unique vista from the shadowy western tip of the *Île de la Cité*, especially as dusk begins to fall, although it is usually crowded at this time. The romantically inclined and dance enthusiasts often picnic on the *quai Saint-Bernard*, (left bank, between Île de la Cité and Austerlitz station). 🐷 There's salsa and tango dancing on the riverfront here in the early evening (free).

Another great spot for a picnic is along the *Canal Saint-Martin* (see p. 53). Picnickers spread out their blankets late into the evening along the romantic, tree-lined waterway, with its quaint bridges and locks, and eat baguettes, cheese, pastries and quiches washed down with cider, wine or beer. A little further north, on the *Canal de l'Ourcq*, people don't only eat, but play boules and its Scandinavian equivalent, *mölkky*.

All in all, picnics are an economical and convivial affair in a typically Parisian atmosphere.

SIGHT SEEING

Whether you're set on visiting the major attractions, on the lookout for the most spectacular squares and expensive shops, or seeking the charm of "old Paris" with its winding lanes, what you make of your stay in Paris is entirely up to you.

In order to provide a better overview, the inner city, known by Parisians as the area "intra muros", has been categorised into six areas in this guidebook. They cover the 20 arrondissements within the Boulevard Périphérique ringroad. Parisians tend to visualise

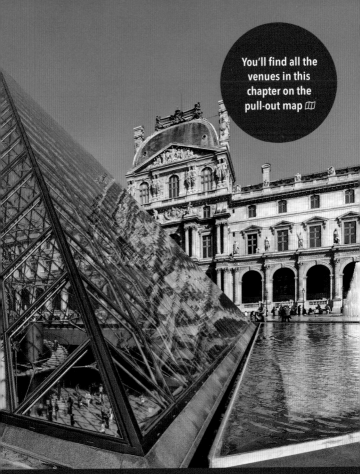

You'll find all the venues in this chapter on the pull-out map 🗺

Temple to the arts: Musée du Louvre

their city in terms of the numbers 1 to 20: ask a Parisian where something is and they'll probably answer with a number. So that you know where to go, our six areas also follow the arrondissements. Just pick the spots that interest you, and off you go!

To prevent your exploration of the city from becoming too much, it's well worth taking a break every now and then, and seeking out one of the magnificent parks and green spaces or relaxing in one of the city's numerous cafés.

CHAMPS-ÉLYSÉES TO THE OPÉRA p. 47

See and be seen

Clichy

Levallois-Perret

Courbevoie

Neuilly-sur-Seine

Puteaux

Gare Saint-Lazare

● Arc de Triomphe ★

Avenue Victor Hugo

Avenues des Champs-Élysées

Bois de Boulogne

Jardins du Trocadéro

Musée d'Orsay ★

● Eiffel Tower ★

Versailles ★

QUARTIER LATIN TO THE EIFFEL TOWER p. 40

Intellectual life and true splendour

Gare Vaugirard

MARCO POLO HIGHLIGHTS

★ **ÎLE DE LA CITÉ**
Still vital and vibrant: the nucleus of the city ➤ p. 30

★ **MUSÉE DU LOUVRE**
The glass pyramid, a Renaissance palace and a museum of superlatives ➤ p. 33

★ **MUSÉE PICASSO**
Perfect palace setting for works by adopted Frenchman Pablo Picasso ➤ p. 36

★ **PLACE DES VOSGES**
The old royal square is one of the oldest in the city ➤ p. 37

★ **CENTRE POMPIDOU**
Futuristic tubular construction, providing a framework for great modern art ➤ p. 38

★ **NOTRE-DAME**
Cathedral saved from the flames: flying buttresses, portals and gargoyles ➤ p. 39

★ **JARDIN DU LUXEMBOURG**
A sumptuous park with a palace in the Florentine style ➤ p. 44

★ **EIFFEL TOWER**
"La Dame en Fer" – The Iron Lady ➤ p. 44

★ **MUSÉE D'ORSAY**
A former Belle-Époque railway station provides the backdrop for Impressionist paintings ➤ p. 46

★ **ARC DE TRIOMPHE**
Gateway honouring the Napoleonic army ➤ p. 48

★ **VERSAILLES**
The imposing palace of Louis XIV, just outside the city ➤ p. 68

MONTMARTRE TO BELLEVILLE p. 60
Trendy artists' and residential quarters

CANAL ST-MARTIN TO BOIS DE VINCENNES p. 51
Multiculturalism for hipsters and party animals

ÎLE DE LA CITÉ TO THE MARAIS p. 30
Paris Centre, the historic heart of the city

MONTPARNASSE TO OIS DE BOULOGNE p. 55
Chinatown meets the French bourgeoisie

Boulevard Ney

Pantin

Gare du Nord

Rue la Fayette

Le Pré-Saint-Gervais

Rue de Châteaudun

Gare de l'Est

Parc des Buttes-Chaumont

Les Lilas

Musée du Louvre ★

Centre Pompidou ★

Musée Picasso ★

Île de la Cité ★   Notre-Dame ★

Place des Vosges ★

Boulevard Saint-Germain

Jardin du Luxembourg ★

Jardin des Plantes

Gare de Lyon

Saint-Mandé

Gare d'Austerlitz

Quai de Bercy

Bois de Vincennes

Charenton-le-Pont

Gentilly

Le Kremlin-Bicêtre

Ivry-sur-Seine

Arcueil

1 km
0.62 mi

To get a real feel for the Parisian way of life, copy the Parisians: people-watching is an activity in itself in this city.

Paris is a city of museums, with well over 100 in total. So you'll have to accept that it's impossible to visit every one, and decide in advance which ones are for you. Anyone who is put off by the sheer size of the sometimes very extensive collections – in the Louvre, you would have to walk some 17km to see everything – can visit one of the many smaller city palaces, which are often veritable treasure troves. Note that most of the city's museums are closed on Mondays, while many national museums are closed on Tuesdays. The Paris Museum Pass (parismuseumpass. com) allows you to visit more than 50 museums and other places of interest (two days: 52 euros, four days: 66 euros, six days: 78 euros). You can obtain the pass at the Office du Tourisme (parisinfo.com), in many of the participating museums or simply online.

Incidentally, many museums are free on the first Sunday of the month, and some sites can be visited 🐖 free of charge all year round. Find out which museums and buildings don't charge for entry on the Paris tourist information website short. travel/par1. Most places offer discounts for schoolchildren, students and senior citizens – EU passport holders under 26, for example, have free admission to all national museums (musées nationaux) in the city. Sometimes you can even skip the queue at the pay desk by showing your ID right at the entrance. Ask about that when you're there.

INSIDER TIP
Free museums!

WHERE TO START?

Paris is large, and there is no easily defined "city centre". For a proper overview, it's best to take the Métro line M 2 to **Anvers station** (📖 L4). As soon as the train is above ground, you'll see Sacré-Coeur in front of you. Once you've scaled the steps, you'll have Paris at your feet. For a close-up of the Île de la Cité and the Louvre, the Métro/RER railway station **Châtelet-Les Halles** (📖 M8) is the ideal starting point.

ÎLE DE LA CITÉ TO THE MARAIS

The first four arrondissements are the heart of Paris. Shaped like a snail, these arrondissements begin in the west of the ⭐ Île de la Cité, where the first inhabitants, the Parisii tribe, settled during the Roman era.

The 1st arrondissement continues along the right bank of the Seine via the "belly of Paris", as writer Émile Zola dubbed the former market halls, with the Westfield Forum des Halles

ÎLE DE LA CITÉ TO THE MARAIS

10 Place Vendôme
7 Musée de l'Orangerie
6 Jardin des Tuileries
5 Carrousel du Louvre
11 Galerie Vivienne
8 Palais Royal & Jardin du Palais Royal
9 Pinault Collection – Bourse de Commerce
12 La Gaîté Lyrique
4 Musée du Louvre ★
17 Centre Pompidou ★
13 Musée Picasso ★
3 Pont Neuf
Hôtel de Ville & Place de l'Hôtel de Ville
Concergerie 2
Sainte-Chapelle 1
Île de la Cité ★
18
Place du Marché Sainte-Cathérine
15
19
16 Place des Vosges ★
14
Maison de Victor Hugo
20 Notre-Dame ★
Maison Européenne de la Photographie
Île Saint-Louis
Jardin du Luxembourg
1 km
0.62 mi

(forumdeshalles.com) shopping centre, the Louvre and the Tuileries to the Place de la Concorde.

The 2nd arrondissement is home to the stock exchange and plenty of geeks. In the former clothworkers' quarter around *rue du Sentier*, very little sewing is done for *haute couture*, with more and more businesses vanishing faced with the pressure of cheaper goods from Asia. Instead, online start-ups have moved in, giving the district its new name "Silicon Sentier". Between Palais Royal and Boulevard Montmartre, make sure to take a look at the shopping arcades dating from the 19th century, which have been restored to varying degrees.

Then it's on to Le Marais in the 3rd and 4th arrondissements. This trendy area with cool gay bars has been a centre of Jewish life since the early 12th century. The *Shoah Memorial (memorialdelashoah.org)* and the *Museum of Jewish Art and History (mahj.org)* bear witness to Jewish history in France. Particularly impressive are the many noble palaces and the *Place des Vosges*, the former royal square. Right to the very south of the 4th arrondissement is the Île Saint-Louis. From here you can reach the Île de la Cité and *Notre-Dame* cathedral.

1 SAINTE-CHAPELLE

This veritable treasure chest of Gothic architecture lies virtually hidden in the courtyard of the central law courts on the Île de la Cité. The 13th-century church houses valuable relics from the Holy Land. The effect of the massive stained-glass windows reaching for the heavens, held together only by filigree buttresses that bathe the entire room in a pale blue light, is breathtaking. The upper floor is the actual chapel and was reserved for the king. *April–Sept daily 9am–7pm, Oct–March daily 9am–5pm | admission 11.50 euros, incl. Conciergerie 18.50 euros (Nov–March 1st Sun of the month free) | 8 bd. du Palais | sainte-chapelle.fr | M 4 Saint-Michel or Cité | 1st arr. | 🚇 L8*

■ CONCIERGERIE

The "antechamber to the guillotine" – as this former prison is rather grimly known – is an imposing structure on the Île de la Cité that chronicles a tragic episode in French history. The most prominent among the more than 2,000 inmates who faced their execution here were Marie Antoinette (her cell has now been reconstructed) and the revolutionaries Georges Danton and Maximilien de Robespierre. The picturesque building, with its rounded towers, was originally a palace of the Capetian ruling dynasty from the 10th century. The *Salle des Gens d'Armes* is considered one of the most impressive examples of Gothic secular architecture. The building's name is derived from the word *concierge*, or chamberlain, who was accorded great power by the king from around 1300 onwards. *Daily 9.30am–6pm | admission 11.50 euros, incl. Sainte-Chapelle 18.50 euros (Nov–March 1st Sun of the month free) | 2 bd du Palais | paris-conciergerie.fr | M 4 Saint-Michel Notre-Dame | 1st arr. | 🚇 L8*

A boat trip on the Seine takes you under the Pont Neuf and past the Île de la Cité

3 PONT NEUF

The "new" bridge that crosses the top of the Île de la Cité is in fact the city's oldest existing bridge. When Henry IV, whose equestrian statue stands atop the structure, inaugurated the bridge in 1607, it was considered highly modern. For the first time in Paris, the view from a bridge of the Seine was unobstructed by houses. It is the most famous crossing point on the Seine – often sung about, the object of countless paintings and the backdrop for many films. The square beneath the equestrian statue provides a magnificent view of the former royal palace, which now houses the world's largest museum. *M 7 Pont Neuf | 1st/6th arr. | ⍰ L8*

INSIDER TIP
A perfect view of the Louvre

4 MUSÉE DU LOUVRE ★

A well-thought-out strategy is required for a visit to the most sprawling museum in the world. After all, there is much more to admire in the Louvre than just the awe-inspiring *Venus of Milo* (second century BCE), Leonardo da Vinci's *Mona Lisa* (16th century) and Jan Vermeer's *The Lacemaker* (17th century). A very helpful map is available in English from the information desk, as is a weekly schedule of room closures for specific collections.

Culture seekers can then choose from a comprehensive range of exhibits dating back to the seventh century BCE that includes eastern, Egyptian and Graeco-Roman civilisations divided among the three building complexes *(Denon, Sully, Richelieu)*. Alongside European sculpture from the Middle Ages to the 19th century, handicrafts and over 100,000 graphic art pieces spanning six centuries, the collection of paintings is quite a highlight. Sub-divided into regions, it documents European painting from the 13th to the 19th centuries. The exuberant stucco, the crown jewels and paintings by Charles Le Brun, Eugène Delacroix and others in the opulent *Apollon-Galerie* bear witness to the immense power of the Sun King, Louis XIV.

Take a break from your museum visit in the aesthetic underground shopping arcade, *Carrousel du Louvre* (see below). Even if you forego a visit to the museum, it is still worthwhile to take a closer look at the Louvre complex, which was transformed from a 12th-century fortress into a Renaissance palace. The exposed *medieval foundations*, the beautifully illuminated (in the evening) *Cour Carée*, the small *triumphal arch* that forms a focal axis with its big brother and the audacious glass *pyramid* by the Chinese architect IM Pei are absolute highlights of any visit to Paris. The *H all Napoléon* in the lobby below the Pyramid hosts special exhibitions.

Tickets must be bought online as no tickets are sold at the automatic ticket machines on site when there are large crowds. *Wed–Mon 9am–6pm (Fri until 9.45pm) | admission 15 euros on site, 17 euros online (free on 14 July) | louvre.fr | M 1, 7 Palais Royal-Musée du Louvre | ⏱ 2.5–4 hrs, or a relaxed whole day | 1st arr. | ⍰ K–L7*

5 CARROUSEL DU LOUVRE ☂

The shopping arcade has only existed since 1990. The passages under the glass pyramid and the Louvre provide a venue for upscale shops as well as restaurants and cafés. This is the ideal place to take cover during a walk on a rainy Sunday or to purchase last-minute gifts for friends and family back home. The *Boutique des Musées Nationaux* offers reproductions of works of art from various French museums, plus a choice selection of cards and books. There are also endless restaurants and cafes to keep up your strength for (window) shopping. An eatery that offers a different style of refreshment after a long stroll is the *Restaurants du Monde (€)*, which serves specialities from all over the world. *Wed–Mon 10am–7pm, Tue 11am–6pm | carrouseldulouvre.com | M 1, 7 Palais Royal-Musée du Louvre | 1st arr. | ⊞ K7*

INSIDER TIP
Underground shopping and food

6 JARDIN DES TUILERIES

Regarded as the "front garden" of the Louvre, this Baroque park has existed in its current form since 1666. It was one of the first to open to the general public and became a model for many others in Europe. Especially notewor-thy are the 18 statues of women by Aristide Maillol, which seem almost surreal peeking out between the care-fully manicured hedges. *M 1, 8, 12 Concorde | M 1 Tuileries | 1st arr. | ⊞ J–K7*

7 MUSÉE DE L'ORANGERIE

The Jardin des Tuileries adjacent to the Louvre is home to the remarkable collection assembled by the art dealer Paul Guillaume, including works by Auguste Renoir, Pablo Picasso, Paul Cézanne, Henri Matisse and Amedeo Modigliani. The highlight is the famous *Nymphéas* (Water Lilies) by Claude Monet, whose eight large compositions adorn the walls in an elliptical form, enhancing the impres-sion of flowing water and light. A combined ticket with the Musée d'Orsay (18 euros) ensures priority in both queues. *Wed–Mon 9am–6pm | admission 12.50 euros (10 euros for max. 2 people accompanying a minor, 1st Sun of the month free) | Jardin des*

Tuileries | musee-orangerie.fr | M 1, 8, 12 Concorde | ⏱ 1.5 hrs | 1st arr. | 🗺 J7

8 PALAIS ROYAL & JARDIN DU PALAIS ROYAL

A historic place of refuge in the turbulent city centre. Shaded by the lime trees, it was once an epicentre of historical significance. Cardinal Richelieu, who had the palace and its surrounding park constructed in 1634, later bequeathed it to Louis XIII. Its subsequent owners, the House of Orléans, expanded it. Behind the uniform façades with rounded, arched arcades, shops can still be found just like centuries ago. The French Revolution began here in July 1789. In the adjacent courtyard next to *La Comédie Française*, the columns of varying heights by Daniel Buren have provided an interesting counterbalance to the historical backdrop since 1986. *Daily from 8am, in summer until late evening | rue Saint-Honoré | domaine-palais-royal.fr | M 1, 7 Palais Royal-Musée du Louvre | 1st arr. | 🗺 K7*

9 PINAULT COLLECTION – BOURSE DE COMMERCE

François Pinault is one of the richest men in France and spent around 150m euros converting the former Paris commodities exchange building into a museum. While the pandemic postponed the opening several times, you can now marvel at contemporary works of art from Pinault's collection in

Designed by André Le Nôtre, the Jardin des Tuileries is a popular public space

Paris as well as Venice. *Wed–Mon 11am–7pm (Fri & first Sat of the month until 9pm) | admission 14 euros (free 1st Sat of the month 5–9pm) | 2 rue de Viarmes | M 4 Les Halles | 1st arr. | ⊞ L6*

⑩ PLACE VENDÔME

This masterpiece of classical symmetry with its characteristic oblique square form on four sides was built at the end of the 17th century by the famous master builder Jules Hardouin-Mansart. A column in the style of a Roman Trojan column stands in the middle of the square, and at its top Napoleon is depicted as a Roman emperor. Place Vendôme is also known world-wide for its renowned jewellers and the famous Hôtel Ritz, which benefits from the location's extraordinary atmosphere. *M 3, 7, 8 Opéra | 1st arr. | ⊞ J–K6*

⑪ GALERIE VIVIENNE ▐

The gallery is considered the queen of Parisian arcades and was completely refurbished at the turn of the millennium. Here, under glass-domed roofs, you can saunter past select shops over the beautiful neo-classical-style mosaics on the floor. After a visit to *Emilio Robba*, where you'll find the most gorgeous artificial flowers in the world, sample an exquisite *chocolat à l'ancienne* at *Le Valentin*. Not far afield is the building of the same vintage, the *Galerie Colbert*, with its Pompeian-style rotunda. *4 rue des Petits Champs | galerie-vivienne.com | M 3 Bourse | 2nd arr. | ⊞ L6*

⑫ LA GAÎTÉ LYRIQUE ☞

Today, this former theatre built in the 19th century is a temple to digital culture. On the docket: concerts, exhibitions, film screenings, brunch. *Tue–Fri 2–8pm, Sat/Sun noon–7pm | 3 bis rue Papin | gaite-lyrique.net | M 3, 4 Réaumur-Sébastopol | 3rd arr. | ⊞ M6*

⑬ MUSÉE PICASSO ★

Some art aficionados claim that Pablo Picasso (1881–1973) was the greatest artist of the 20th century. The Picasso museum in Marais holds the largest collection of his works, with 5,000 pieces. Make sure to take a look at the artist's private collection, including works by Henri Matisse, Edgar Degas, Georges Braque, Joan Miró and others. You will need plenty of time for this first-rate museum and the stately *Hôtel Salé* in which it is housed. *Tue–Fri 10.30am–6pm, Sat/Sun 9.30am–6pm | admission 14 euros (11 euros for max. 2 people accompanying a minor, 1st Sun of the month free) | 5 rue de Thorigny | museepicasso paris.fr | M 8 Saint-Sébastien-Froissart | ⊙ 1/2 day | 3rd arr. | ⊞ N7*

⑭ MAISON DE VICTOR HUGO

The writer Victor Hugo lived and worked here between 1832 and 1848. Some of the rooms have an Asian influence. Here, you not only have a wonderful view of the Place des Vosges, but you can also marvel at the poet's documents, objects, furniture and paintings, which reveal he was also a very good painter – he left numerous paintings and around

3,000 drawings. *Tue–Sun 10am–6pm | free admission (temporary exhibitions 6–9 euros) | 6 pl. des Vosges | maisonsvictorhugo.paris.fr | M 1 Saint-Paul | ⏱ 1–2 hrs | 4th arr. | 🕮 O8*

🔢 PLACE DU MARCHÉ SAINTE-CATHÉRINE

The cafés and shady trees of this quiet location in Marais will remind you of a tranquil marketplace in a provincial town in the South of France, especially in summer. *M 1 Saint-Paul | 4th arr. | 🕮 N8*

🔢 PLACE DES VOSGES ★

At the beginning of the 17th century, King Henry IV commissioned what was originally known as the Place Royale. It is not only one of the oldest, but also one of the most architecturally harmonious squares in the city. The 36 pavilions or houses (those of the king and queen are slightly higher) are framed by arcades where elegant art galleries and restaurants are now housed. Above these, the symmetrically arranged façades with their composition of light natural stone, red-brick facing and grey slated roofs create a perfect picture. The uniformity of the ensemble is best appreciated from the small park in the centre of the square. *Marais | M 1 Saint-Paul, M 1, 5, 8 Bastille | 4th arr. | 🕮 N–O8*

Place des Vosges: a fountain stands at the heart of this harmonious ensemble of buildings

17 CENTRE POMPIDOU ★

The fourth and fifth levels of this futuristic tubular structure give you a comprehensive overview of 20th-century art. The interdisciplinary approach to graphic art, architecture, design and new media is fascinating. A true-to-life replica of the studio of the famous sculptor Constantin Brancusi is situated on the forecourt outside the building. On the sixth level, temporary exhibits of works by world-renowned artists are displayed. It's worth a visit for the phenomenal view of Paris alone. A lift to the left of the main entrance will take you straight to the top floor free of charge. If you're not in the mood for art, you can also enjoy a drink at the designer café *Georges (restaurant georgesparis.com)*.

INSIDER TIP
Cheers, here's to good health!

Next to the Centre is a fountain, with water-spraying sculptures by Niki de Saint Phalle and Jean Tinguely in a tribute to the ballet *Le Sacre du Printemps* by Igor Stravinsky, characterised by its colourful figures and technical contraptions. *Wed–Mon 11am–9pm (Thu temporary exhibitions until 11pm), Atelier Brancusi 2pm–6pm | admission 14 euros, Atelier Brancusi free (1st Sun of the month free) | Place Georges-Pompidou |*

Fontaine Strawinsky by Niki de Saint Phalle and Jean Tinguely

centrepompidou.fr | M 11 Rambuteau |
⏱ 2–3 hrs | 4th arr. | ⧠ M7

🔞 HÔTEL DE VILLE & PLACE DE L'HÔTEL DE VILLE

This has been the seat of Paris's city government since the middle ages. The current *city hall*, designed in neo-Renaissance style, was constructed after the previous building was destroyed in an act of arson during the Paris Commune of 1871. Today, the only type of executions that take place in front of the building are verbal ones – the square is still a space for protests, as well as for fairs and sporting events. Parisians primarily

flock to the city hall to view the free, rotating exhibitions hosted here. For security reasons, tours are no longer being offered. *11 Hôtel de Ville | M 4, 7, 11, 14 Châtelet | 4th arr. | ⧠ M8*

🔞 MAISON EUROPÉENNE DE LA PHOTOGRAPHIE

This grand 18th-century villa is home to contemporary photography – rotating exhibitions of manageable size on a specific subject, movement or artist. Parisians attend the exhibitions often and repeatedly. *Wed/Fri 11am–8pm, Thur 11am–10pm, Sat/Sun 10am–8pm | admission 10 euros | 5–7 rue de Fourcy | mep-fr.org | M 1 Saint-Paul | ⏱ 1–2 hrs | 4th arr. | ⧠ N8*

🔟 NOTRE-DAME ★

Images of the burning cathedral, its spire in danger of collapse, flew around the world on 15 April 2019. But in an operation lasting several hours, the fire brigade was able to save the cathedral. Within a few days, donations of almost one billion euros had poured in to rebuild Notre-Dame, and the cathedral is to be restored to its former glory in time for the 2024 Olympic Games.

This Gothic masterpiece was built between 1163 and 1345 at the instigation of Bishop Maurice de Sully. A Roman temple had once stood on the square 2,000 years before. The interior of the five-aisled nave can accommodate 9,000 people. The three large entrance portals, the massive flying buttresses around the choir, and the rose windows with a diameter of over 32 feet are especially impressive.

QUARTIER LATIN TO THE EIFFEL TOWER

Many historically significant events have taken place here, including Napoleon's coronation. During the revolution, Notre-Dame was transformed into a "temple of reason" and the church seemed to be in danger of demise. In his book *The Hunchback of Notre-Dame*, Victor Hugo successfully appealed to the public to stop tolerating the situation, and the cathedral was restored as a result. In the forecourt, which will be given a green makeover as part of the renovations, there is a special marking from which distances to other French cities can be measured.

By some miracle, the majority of the sculptures to adorn the facades and the Cavaillé-Coll organ all survived the fire. Until each and every organ pipe is cleaned and the free concerts resume on a Saturday evening *(musique-sacree-notredame deparis.fr)*, in the *Saint Eustache church (146 rue Rambuteau | M 4 Les Halles | sainteustache.org | 1st arr. | ⌨ L7)* you can enjoy 🎵 organ music free of charge every Sunday before the 10.45am and 5pm services.

INSIDER TIP
The divine sound of the organ

The cathedral's shop has already reopened before renovation work to the forecourt is complete and tours, both around the cathedral and virtual, are also on offer again. *Parvis Notre-Dame-Place Jean-Paul II, Île de la Cité | notredamedeparis.fr, tours-notre-dame-de-paris.fr | M 4 Cité or St-Michel, RER B, C Saint-Michel-Notre-Dame | 4th arr. | ⌨ M9*

The 5th, 6th and 7th arrondissements are the three central districts south of the Seine. The Latin quarter and Saint-Germain-des-Prés, in the 5th and 6th arrondissements, have always been a centre for the intelligentsia.

Back in the 1950s the existentialists would meet in the cafés here, though today the area is more popular with tourists and the staff from surrounding offices and shops. The Quartier Latin (where Latin was once spoken) has housed the most famous educational institutions of the nation since the 13th century, as well as plenty of cafés and bistros, and one of the most popular parks in Paris, the Jardin du Luxembourg.

The 7th arrondissement between the Eiffel Tower and Les Invalides, on the other hand, is firmly in the hands of the upper middle classes – much like the entire western part of the city. The elegant streets, home to the French National Assembly, many prestigious consulates, ministries and several beautiful palaces, are relatively calm and the pace more leisurely. Tourists crowd around this area to see the Eiffel Tower, the city's major landmark, but the area isn't short of museums either. Head to the Champ de Mars in front of the Eiffel Tower and the Esplanade des Invalides

IDER TIP

Why make that big climb?

between the Seine and Les Invalides for a spot on the grass. A picnic in front of the famous tower will prove a lot more relaxing than attempting to climb to the top of it – especially if you haven't booked in advance!

21 INSTITUT DU MONDE ARABE

The striking glass and aluminium façade of the Institut du Monde Arabe, designed by Jean Nouvel, follows the curve of the Seine. A modern take on traditional arabesque-style *mashrebiya* windows have slats that open and close according to the fall of the light. To promote cultural exchange between the European and Islamic world, 20 Arab nations present forums, films and exhibitions here, and there is also an extensive library. The 🐦 free roof terrace and restaurant offer a spectacular view over the roofs of the metropolis. *Tue–Fri 10am–6pm, Sat/Sun 10am–7pm | admission 8 euros | 1 rue des Fossés Saint-Bernard | imarabe.org | M 7, 10 Jussieu | 5th arr. | ᒧ N9*

22 MUSÉE DE CLUNY

The late Gothic city palace of the abbots of Cluny provides an ideal setting for this display of medieval art. As well as the illuminated manuscripts, furniture, crafted pieces and medieval sculptures, the stained-glass windows and wall tapestries are especially stunning. The round salon with six wall tapestries of the *Lady with the Unicorn* (15th century) is a highlight.

While the first five tapestries are allegories of the five senses, the meaning of the sixth inscribed only with "Mon seul désir" (my sole desire) remains a mystery. *Tue–Sun 9.30am–6.15pm | admission 12 euros (1st Sun of the month free) | 6 pl. Paul Painlevé | musee-moyenage.fr | M 10 Cluny-La Sorbonne | ☉ medieval history fans should plan to spend a morning | 5th arr. | ᒧ L9*

Institut du Monde Arabe

QUARTIER LATIN TO THE EIFFEL TOWER

23 PANTHÉON

This massive domed structure can be seen from a distance on the hill of Sainte-Geneviève. Louis XV had the edifice constructed in 1756 by his master builder Jacques-Germain Soufflot in fulfillment of a vow to Geneviève, the patron saint of Paris. Shortly after the Revolution, the church became the final resting place of French luminaries such as Voltaire and Jean-Jacques Rousseau. Since Victor Hugo's body was transferred to the Panthéon in 1885, the building – which is still occasionally used as a place of worship – was finally considered a mausoleum. You can scale the stairs to the gallery of the dome from which the physicist Léon Foucault conducted his famous pendulum experiment, demonstrating the earth's rotational axis. *April–Sept daily 10am–6.30pm, Oct–March daily 10am–6pm | admission 9 euros (Nov–March 1st Sun of the month free) | Place du Panthéon | paris-pantheon.fr | M 10 Cardinal Lemoine, RER B Luxembourg |* ⏱ *1 hr | 5th arr. |* ⊞ *L10*

24 RUE MOUFFETARD ⚑

This little street has wound its way down the vibrant Montagne Sainte-Geneviève since Roman times. Tourists and locals treasure the narrow lane, with its small bars and boutiques, and well-stocked market (Tue–Sun) at its lower end. The scenic *Place de la Contrescarpe* with its lovely cafés is located at the upper end of the "Mouff". *M 7 Place Monge | 5th arr. |* ⊞ *M10–11*

25 MUSÉE DE LA SCULPTURE EN PLEIN AIR

Open-air sculpture free of charge in the *Jardin Tino-Rossi* on the banks of the Seine. Discover around 30 works by sculptors including César Baldaccini and Constantin Brancusi as you walk around. *Quai Saint-Bernard | M 7, 10 Jussieu | ⏲ 30 mins | 5th arr. | 🕮 N9–10*

26 JARDIN DES PLANTES

The Jardin des Plantes (summer 7.30am–8pm, winter 8am–5.30pm, times vary depending on the season) offers a free educational garden and is also home to the National Museum of Natural History *(Muséum National d'Histoire Naturelle, mnhn.fr)*. Children will definitely want to start with the *Ménagerie (depending on the season Mon–Sat 10am–5/6pm, Sun 10am–6.30pm | admission 13 euros, under 25s 10 euros, under 3s free | ⏲ 1–2 hrs)*, a zoo with reptiles, monkeys and big cats. Another way to learn more about science is to head to the museum's *Grande Galerie de l'Évolution (daily 10am–6pm | admission from 10 euros, under 25s free | ⏲ 2 hrs)* on another site within the Jardin des Plantes. The caravan of life-sized stuffed animals is particularly impressive. Head to the other side of the Jardin for *Palaeontology (daily 10am–6pm | admission 10 euros, under 25s free | ⏲ 1–2 hrs)* for more wonders including huge dinosaur bones, or enjoy *mineralogy (daily 10am–6pm | admission from 7 euros, under 25s free | ⏲ | 1–2 hrs)*. The greenhouses *Les Grandes Serres (daily summer 10am–6pm, winter 10am–5pm | admission 7 euros, under 25s*

Piles and piles of beautiful seafood on rue Mouffetard

5 euros, under 3s free | ⏱ 1.5 hrs) house lush jungle flora and are just magnificent. ☞ You can buy a three-day ticket valid for all areas for 25 euros. *jardindesplantesdeparis.fr | M 5, 10, RER C Gare d'Austerlitz | 5th arr. | ⏱ N10*

☷ JARDIN DU LUXEMBOURG ★

The most famous park in the centre of Paris is quite close to the Sorbonne. You can watch children sailing 🚣 boats in the large pond from one of the available, and famous, Fermob chairs. This has been a favourite pastime of little Parisians since 1881 *(daily in summer & French school holidays 11am–6pm, otherwise Sat/ Sun 11am–6pm, Wed 1pm–6pm, closed in winter | 6 euros/30 mins | lesvoiliersduluxembourg.fr).* Maria de' Medici had the park and palace constructed at the beginning of the 17th century as an imitation of her native Florence. The *Palais du Luxembourg* is the headquarters of the French Senate today. The adjacent *Musée du Luxembourg (museeduluxembourg. fr)* often has exceptional art exhibitions. *Park: depending on the season 7.30/8.15am until 1 hr before sunset | RER B Luxembourg | 6th arr. | ⏱ K–L 9–10*

☷ EIFFEL TOWER (TOUR EIFFEL) ★

Paris would not be Paris without the Eiffel Tower. The 300m-high landmark long held the distinction of being the highest structure in the world. Built by Gustave Eiffel on the occasion of the 100-year anniversary of the French Revolution and the World Exposition in 1889, the steel structure was initially highly controversial. The tower was originally only meant to stay in place for 20 years. But, because of its importance as a weather station and later for air traffic, as well as a radio and television station, it was allowed to remain.

The second platform, at a height of 115m, provides an impressive panoramic view over Paris; from the highest level, at 274m, the view on a clear day extends right across the whole Paris basin. If you want to, you can sip a glass of champagne on the platform (from 15 euros). In 2018, glass walls were installed around the Eiffel Tower to prevent terrorist attacks.

If you aren't content with seeing the famous tower from below, be sure to book in advance online. You can book tickets with a fixed time slot to save yourself queueing on the ground. Or for something really special, make a reservation at one of the restaurants and enjoy the privilege of a private lift that takes you to the chic (and expensive) Jules Verne on the second floor. At lunchtime, the *Madame Brasserie (restaurants-toureiffel.com)* on the first floor is open to the general public without a reservation. Entrance to the tower is included with your reservation. *Daily 9/9.30am–11.45pm/ 12.45am | Lift/stairs: 2nd floor 17.10/10.70 euros, 3rd floor 26.80/ 20.40 euros | 5 av. Gustave Eiffel | toureiffel.paris | RER C Champ de Mars – Tour Eiffel | ⏱ 2–3 hrs | 7th arr. | ⏱ F8*

INSIDER TIP
Want to go t the top?

29 MUSÉE DU QUAI BRANLY – JACQUES CHIRAC ⚓

Even from outside, this museum, designed by architect Jean Nouvel, looks quite impressive. The vertical garden created by botanist Patrick Blanc and consisting of 15,000 plants, is especially remarkable. Inside, the journey takes you to distant lands and provides an extensive overview of non-European art. The exhibitions are attractively displayed with numerous multimedia installations. Special events such as theatre, dance and music performances are also held regularly, and shouldn't be missed. Recommended: the museum's restaurant *Les Ombres* (see p. 78). *Tue–Sun 10.30am–7pm (Thu until 10pm) | admission 12 euros (free 1st Sun of the month) | 37 Quai Branly | quaibranly.fr | M 9 Iéna, RER C Pont de l'Alma | ⏱ at least half a day | 7th arr. | 🗺 F7*

30 LES INVALIDES

The *Hôtel des Invalides* is, the second largest building complex constructed during the reign of Louis XIV, after Versailles. The Sun King had it built for his wounded war veterans. In order to prevent the ex-soldiers from becoming beggars or thieves, he set up special workshops governed by strict discipline to provide up to 3,000 invalids with work and good care. In addition to the soldiers' church, the *Dôme des Invalides* with its shining golden cupola is the main attraction. *Napoleon's tomb* reigns over the area beneath the dome. The annexed *Army Museum*, founded in 1794, is one of

Napoleon's final resting place, with its six interlocking coffins, is in the Dôme des Invalides

Great art in an old railway station: sculptures in the main hall of the Musée d'Orsay

the largest of its kind in the world. *Daily 10am–6pm | admission 14 euros | Esplanade des Invalides | musee-armee.fr | M 8 La Tour-Maubourg, M 13 Varenne | ⏲ 1–2 hrs | 7th arr. | ⬚ G–H8*

🟥 MUSÉE RODIN

It was none other than the German poet Rainer Maria Rilke, who temporarily worked as Auguste Rodin's private secretary for a period of eight months in 1905/6, who persuaded him to settle in this grand city palace. In addition to his famous works such as *The Kiss* or *The Cathedral*, some

pieces by his gifted pupil and lover, Camille Claudel, can also be seen here. The adjoining sculpture park and café are a perfect place to relax, surrounded by art. *Tue–Sun 10am–6.30pm | admission 13 euros (Oct–March 1st Sun of the month free), combi ticket with the Musée d'Orsay 24 euros | 77 rue de Varenne | musee-rodin.fr | M 13 Varenne | ⏲ incl. park, at least 3 hrs | 7th arr. | ⬚ H8*

🟥 MUSÉE D'ORSAY ⭐ 🚩

The painters of light, the Impressionists, form the focal point in the light-flooded rooms of this former railway station, which was converted in 1986. Works by the precursors of modernist painting such as Vincent van Gogh, Paul Gauguin and Paul Cézanne can also be admired. The paintings, sculptures, and *objets d'art*, as well as urban planning documentation, and film and film poster art, cover the period from 1848 to 1914, one of the most fruitful epochs in art history. Not only is the museum bookshop's extensive selection impressive, but so is the elegant restaurant, where the modern seating harmonises well with the splendour of the Belle-Époque era. *Tue–Sun 9.30am–6pm (Thu until 9.45pm) | admission 16 euros (1st Sun of the month free) | 1 rue de la Légion d'Honneur | musee-orsay.fr | RER C Musée d'Orsay | ⊙ various 1.5 hour tours on the website, otherwise half a day | 7th arr. | ▥ J7*

CHAMPS-ÉLYSÉES TO THE OPÉRA

The famed and prestigious Champs-Elysées forms part of a vista which runs from the small arch of the Carrousel du Louvre, continues to the middle arch of the Arc de Triomphe and then ends to the west at the giant, modern Grande Arche de La Défense.

Traffic on the multiple-lane *grand boulevard* is hectic day and night, and only comes to a standstill on one Sunday a month. Then pandemonium also rules among the masses of tourists who spill out onto the broad pavements throughout the year. In the boutiques, some of which are open until midnight, and in the numerous cafés, the motto "see and be seen" prevails. In order to uphold the boulevard's upmarket image, the city authorities have adopted a policy limiting the number of cheap chain stores that are permitted to trade in this coveted area. The *grand boulevard* is intersected at the lower end by the avenue Montaigne, one of the most expensive addresses when it comes to fashion. The glass palaces, the Grand and Petit Palais, erected in 1900 on the occasion of the World Exposition, are located in this section, which is lined by luxuriant greenery. The Palais de la Découverte *(palais-decouverte. fr)*, which now houses a science museum, is here too.

If you're heading for Place de la Concorde, don't forget to make a detour to the right of the Louvre in the direction of *Pont Alexandre III*. From this vantage point you can really appreciate the splendour so typical of the Napoleonic era and the Belle Époque. If you're game for another round of sightseeing, cross the Place de la Concorde and stroll down the elegant rue Royale to the *church of Sainte-Marie Madeleine (La Madeleine)* and from there on to the old opera house *(Opéra Garnier)*. If your appetite for sightseeing still isn't satiated, take a stroll along *rue des Martyrs* in South Pigalle, or SoPi, as the trendy district likes to market itself.

CHAMPS-ÉLYSÉES TO THE OPÉRA

33 ARC DE TRIOMPHE ★

The 50m-high Parisian landmark created by Jean François Chalgrin, based on buildings from antiquity, rises up along the impressive axis drawn between the small arch of the Louvre and the large arch of La Défense. After Napoleon commissioned the building in 1806 in honour of his "great army" and his victory at the Battle of Austerlitz, it took another 30 years until it was finished. Under the arch, which features important reliefs, including *La Marseillaise*, you will find the *Tombe du Soldat Inconnu* (Tomb of the Unknown Soldier), the starting point for the military parade held every year on 14 July.

An underground passage near the Métro station at the Place Charles de Gaulle-Étoile leads past a small museum on the history of the Arc de Triomphe to the entrance to the viewing platform. You should by no means miss this phenomenal view: no less than a dozen avenues radiate out from the monument in the shape of a star. *Daily 10am–11pm* |*13 euros (Nov– March 1st Sun of the month free)* | *arc-de-triomphe.monuments-nationaux.fr* | *M 1, 2, 6, RER A Charles de Gaulle-Etoile* | ⏱ *1 hr* | *8th arr.* | ▢ *F5*

34 AVENUE DES CHAMPS-ELYSÉES

The supposedly most beautiful street in the world is not particularly appreciated by Parisians, which is why it is mostly teeming with tourists between the Arc de Triomphe and Place de la Concorde. There are lengthy queues of tourists and locals alike in the evenings and especially at weekends in front of the large cinemas featuring premieres. While the upper part of the avenue consists of fast-food chains and other contemporary commercial outlets, the magnificence of the Belle Époque is more evident further down.

A short detour to the *Avenue de Marigny* leads you directly to the front of the Elysée Palace, the president's residence. Famous addresses on the mile-long *grand boulevard* are the elegant perfumery *Guérlain (no. 68)*, the renowned dance theatre *Le Lido de Paris (no. 116)*, as well as the exclusive boutique *Louis Vuitton (no. 101)*. M 1 George V, M 1, 9 Franklin D. Roosevelt, M 1, 13 Champs-Elysées-Clemenceau | *8th arr.* | ᗰ F–H 5–6

ᗷ AVENUE MONTAIGNE 🏴

The city's stretch of luxury boutiques, a side street of the Champs-Elysées, is where you'll find nearly every notable fashion designer (Versace, Chanel, Dior), jewellers, perfumeries and leather goods stores. It is not uncommon for customers to be brought to the entrance by their chauffeurs, where they are then greeted by white-gloved porters.

If you can afford to stay in a luxury hotel, try the traditional *Plaza Athénée*. You will also find the *Théâtre des Champs-Elysées (no. 15)* with its beautiful façade designed by Antoine Bourdelle on this street. *M 1, 9 Franklin D. Roosevelt* | *8th arr.* | ᗰ G6

Enjoy the flair of the Champs-Élysées from a seat at restaurant L'Alsace

🟥 GRAND & PETIT PALAIS

Both palaces were constructed for the 1900 World Exposition, and their opulent and historicised decorative sculptures symbolise one of the most flourishing cultural epochs of Paris. The iron-and-glass construction and domes are jewels of Art Nouveau and Belle Époque style. The *Grand Palais (opening hours vary | 3 av. du Général Eisenhower | grandpalais.fr)* hosts high-profile events and temporary exhibitions and will be fully renovated by 2025. Until then, a temporary Grand Palais is in place on the Champ de Mars. The lavishly restored *Petit Palais (Tue–Sun 10am–6pm, Fri until 9pm | av. Winston Churchill | petit palais.paris.fr)* has a permanent exhibition with artworks and paintings from the 18th and 19th centuries *(free admission, temporary exhibitions 8–16 euros). M 1, 13 Champs-Elysées-Clemenceau | ⏱ 2 hrs | 8th arr. | ⌖ H6*

🟥 PONT ALEXANDRE III 🏴

Tsar Nicholas II personally laid the foundation for the city's most magnificent bridge, which connects the Grand Palais and the Esplanade des Invalides, in 1896. In sunny weather the gold of the winged Belle-Époque horses shimmering on the bridge's corner pillars can be seen from far and wide. *M 8, 13, RER C Invalides | 7th/8th arr. | ⌖ H7*

🟥 JEU DE PAUME

Don't let the exterior fool you! This grand 19th-century gymnasium is anything but old-fashioned. Rotating exhibits bring 20th- and 21st-century

The beautiful Pont Alexandre III is one of 35 bridges to span the Seine in the city

imagery to life. You can also view photography, video and internet art in the museum's virtual gallery on its website at *"Création en ligne"*. *Tue–Fri noon–8pm, Sat/Sun 11am–7pm | admission 12 euros | 1 Place de la Concorde | jeudepaume.org | M 1, 8, 12 Concorde |* ⏱ *1.5 hrs | 8th arr. |* 🗺 *J6*

39 PLACE DE LA CONCORDE

The most monumental square in Paris is superlative in every way: you have the entire Champs-Elysées up to the Arc de Triomphe before your very eyes from its centre point, the 3,300 year-old, 22m-high Egyptian obelisk. It is hard to imagine that, on this very square built in 1775, thousands of opponents of the Revolution – including Louis XVI and his wife, Marie-Antoinette, as well as Robespierre and the Countess du Barry, met their deaths here by guillotine. The eight female statues framing the Place de la Concorde represent the eight largest cities in France. *M 1, 8, 12 Concorde | 8th arr. |* 🗺 *J6–7*

40 LA MADELEINE

Originally planned as a victory hall for the Grande Armée, this building was ultimately converted into a "modest" church after Napoleon's defeat in Russia. Today, Parisians come to the newly renovated *Sainte-Marie Madeleine* – which was modelled after ancient temples – not only to attend church services, but more often to take in one of the numerous classical concerts (admission around 30 euros, but many concerts are 🐷 free of charge).

Daily 9.30am–7pm | Place de la Madeleine | eglise-lamadeleine.com | M 8, 12, 14 Madeleine | 8th arr. | 🗺 *J6*

41 OPÉRA GARNIER

This sumptuous palace laden with marble and gold is the place to watch opera and ballet. The opera house was completed by Charles Garnier in 1875, with ceiling paintings created by Marc Chagall in 1964. Want to learn more? Take a guided tour! *Daily 10am–5pm, summer until 6pm | admission 12–20 euros | Place de l'Opéra | M 3, 7, 8 Opéra, RER A Auber | operadeparis.fr |* ⏱ *1.5 hrs | 9th arr. |* 🗺 *K5*

CANAL ST-MARTIN TO BOIS DE VINCENNES

The 10th arrondissement welcomes many travellers from the UK, with both Gare du Nord and Gare de l'Est close by. And word has long since spread that there are more than just train stations to explore here: the area also encompasses the district around Canal Saint-Martin.

Around the Métro station Strasbourg-Saint-Denis, along *rue du Faubourg Saint-Denis*, is a nightlife hotspot. Here, the city isn't so much chic and elegant as loud and raucous. Watch the video of "S.S.D"

There are five locks to navigate on the Canal Saint-Martin

(Strasbourg-Saint-Denis) by French rock band La Femme for a pretty good insight into what you can expect here. While people party the night away in the local bars, prostitutes wait outside for customers.

The 11th arrondissement, while still a hotspot of Parisian nightlife, is a little more restrained. Here, the area around *rue Oberkampf* and in the shadow of the Opéra Bastille, around the *rue du Faubourg Saint-Antoine* on the border with the 12th arrondissement, are the places to party.

The three main squares – *Place de la République*, *Place de la Bastille* and *Place de la Nation* – have all been extensively rebuilt in recent years.

Once only accessible when closed for a demonstration (you are in the heart of revolutionary Paris, after all!), the multi-lane thoroughfares are now reserved for pedestrians and cyclists.

The 12th arrondissement, once home to craftspeople and furniture dealers, is now a business district and home to the Ministry of the Economy. But that doesn't mean it's devoid of culture thanks to the new opera house *(Opéra Bastille)*, the *Cinematèque* and the stadium *(Accor Arena)*, whose name was sold by the city much to the locals' chagrin. If you can spare the time, be sure to walk along the *Coulée verte René-Dumont* to the *Bois de Vincennes*.

42 GARE DE L'EST MODEL RAILWAY 👥

Hidden under the Gare de l'Est are three miniature railway networks belonging to the *Association Française des Amis des Chemins de fer*. This is where retired railway staff and other enthusiasts run model trains. 🐷 On Saturday afternoons, they open up this quaint place to the public free of charge and the people there are more than happy to answer questions with patience and have countless anecdotes to tell. Like the one about the German officer who is said to have stolen parts here during World War II to give to high-ranking Nazi Hermann Göring. *Sat 3–6pm (closed Aug) | free admission | Gare de l'Est, Parking Alsace, Porte 9 | short.travel/par11 | M 4, 5, 7 Gare de l'Est | ⏱ 1/2 hr | 10th arr. | ⎕ N5*

43 CANAL SAINT-MARTIN 👥

Of course you can picnic on the Saint-Martin canal, but did you know you can also navigate it too? It takes 2.5 hours to sail from the *Musée d'Orsay* (see p. 46) through locks, tunnels and under bridges to the *Parc de la Villette*. *Every day in high season | departures 10am & 3pm from Quai Anatole France or 2.30pm from Parc de la Villette | fare 22 euros, children 4–14 14 euros, 15–25s 19 euros | pariscanal.com | ⏱ 2.5 hrs | 10th/19th arr. | ⎕ N-O 4-6*

44 LE QUADRILATÈRE DE L'HÔPITAL SAINT-LOUIS

Tucked away behind the Saint-Louis hospital not far from the Canal Saint-Martin lies a small oasis from another era! The original walls were built in the early 17th century to keep plague patients isolated from the healthy. If the square courtyard reminds you of the Place des Vosges (see p. 37), you're not far off: Henri IV's architects worked on both squares. Besides patients and hospital staff, families from the area love to relax on the spacious lawns with the large, shady trees. *Daily 11am–6pm | 1 av. Claude-Vellefaux | M 11 Goncourt | 10th arr. | ⎕ O5*

CANAL ST-MARTIN TO BOIS DE VINCENNES

43 Canal Saint-Martin
Parc des Buttes-Chaumo
R. La Fayette
42 Model Railway Gare de l'Est
Blvd. de Magenta
Canal Saint-Martin
44 Le Quadrilatère de l'Hôpital Saint-Louis
Rue de Belleville
Blvd. de Belleville
43 Canal Saint-Martin
Ave. de la République
46 Musée Edith Piaf
Blvd. Voltaire
45 Atelier des Lumières
Blvd. Beaumarchais
R. Saint-Antoine
47 Opéra Bastille
Boulevard Henri IV
48 Coulée verte René-Dum
1 km
0.62 mi

Bastille: not a prison, but an opera house

45 ATELIER DES LUMIÈRES 🏛

This former foundry sees you stand not just in front of the most diverse works of art, but right in the middle of them, as artistic classics are reinvented for the digital world! State-of-the-art 3D technology and over 100 video projectors bring these visions to life. *Sept–June Mon–Thu 10am–6pm, Fri/Sat 10am–10pm, Sun 10am–7pm, July/Aug Mon–Sat 10am–8pm | admission 18 euros, 5–25s 13 euros (or 16 or 11 euros respectively online) | 38 rue Saint-Maur | atelier-lumieres.com | M 3 rue Saint-Maur | ⏱ 1 hr | 11th arr. | ▭ P7*

46 MUSÉE EDITH PIAF

This museum is hidden in the tiny flat that once housed the singer in the early days of her career. Pictures, objects and clothing bring Piaf back to life. *Mon–Wed 1–6pm, Thu 10am–noon | by appointment only: tel. 01 43 55 52 72 | free admission | 5 rue Crespin du Gast | M 2 Ménilmontant | ⏱ 45 mins | 11th arr. | ▭ P6*

47 OPÉRA BASTILLE

The silvery façade of glass, steel and granite on the Place de la Bastille is hard to miss. Canadian architect Carlos Ott constructed the new opera house in 1989. Even if you do not want to attend any of the opera or ballet performances, it is still worth the 1½-hour tour *(info on the website). Admission 17 euros | Place de la Bastille | operade-paris.fr | M 1, 5, 8 Bastille | ⏱ 1.5 hrs | 12th arr. | ▭ O9*

48 COULÉE VERTE RENÉ-DUMONT

What the High Line is to New Yorkers, the Coulée Verte is to Parisians: closed to trains in 1969, this former railway line now offers the opportunity to walk 4.5 km from the *Place de la Bastille* through the 12th arrondissement towards the sprawling *Bois de Vincennes* city forest. This green oasis was designed in the late 1980s by landscape architects Philippe Mathieux and Jacques Vergely and is the perfect spot to escape the hustle and bustle of the city for a moment (see Discovery Tour 5). Start at *44-46 rue de Lyon*, where a staircase leads up to the *Viaduc des Arts*, with its approximately 130 shops (see p. 100). *Summer 7/8am-9.30pm, winter 8/9am-5.45pm* | *M 1, 5, 8 Bastille* | ⏱ *1.5-3 hrs* | *12th arr.* | 🗺 *O-Q 9-10*

MONTPARNASSE TO BOIS DE BOULOGNE

Arrondissements 13 to 16 stretch from east to west in the south of Paris. The further west you go, the more chic these residential areas become.

Formerly a working class-area, the 13th arrondissement is just the place if you want to break away from the tourist crowds, and is known for its Chinatown around the *avenue de Choisy*. Fortunately, President Valéry Giscard d'Estaing put a stop to the construction of the uniform concrete blocks you see here as soon as he was elected. Unfortunately, about 30 or so had already been built and now loom as high-rises on the skyline. The four towers of the *National Library* were down to his successor, François Mitterrand.

Next door, the 14th arrondissement is home to the city's second tallest building after the Eiffel Tower: *La Tour Montparnasse*, which is due to be fully renovated by 2024. Continuing the theme of modern architectural sins, we move to Paris' largest arrondissement, the 15th, where things are solid and familiar. Head for the *Beaugrenelle* district to see Corbusier's "vertical city" realised in practice.

Over in the 16th arrondissement, make sure to take another look at the Eiffel Tower. The best spot to snap a picture of the tower is from the forecourt of the *Palais de Chaillot* on the other side of the Seine. Fans of architecture absolutely must make a detour to the *Cité de l'Architecture et du Patrimoine (citedelarchitecture.fr)* for an insight into important French buildings and architects from the 12th century onwards.

INSIDER TIP
Best photo spot for a top Paris shot

49 BIBLIOTHÈQUE NATIONALE DE FRANCE

Interested in modern architecture? Then head for the four glass towers shaped like open books surrounding a little copse near the banks of the

MONTPARNASSE TO BOIS DE BOULOGNE

- **59** Jardin d'Acclimatation
- **58** Fondation Louis Vuitton
- **57** Bois de Boulogne
- Palais de Tokyo **54 55** Musée d'Art Moderne de la Ville de Paris
- Musée Marmottan **53**
- Le Corbusier **56**
- **52** Île aux Cygnes
- Parc des Buttes-Chaumont
- Jardin du Luxembourg
- Montparnasse **51**
- **50** Les Catacombes
- Bibliothèque Nationale de France **49**

2 km
1.24 mi

Seine since 1996. *Temporary exhibitions Tue–Sat 10am–7pm, Sun 1pm–7pm, Library Tue–Sat 10am–8pm, Sun 1–7pm | admission to the reference library 3.90 euros/day, free from 5pm, special exhibits 9 euros | Quai François Mauriac | bnf.fr | M 14, RER C Bibliothèque François Mitterrand | 13th arr. | ◻ P12*

50 LES CATACOMBES ☂

Stone was extracted from underground quarries and used for Paris's buildings. What was left was a network of over 300km of underground passageways. Since Parisian cemeteries were overcrowded until the 18th century, the bones of previous generations were decoratively piled up in these catacombs. Some Parisians use them for illegal parties, but they are

also open for tours. *Tue–Sun 9.45am–8.30pm, last admission 7.30pm, often very long queue times! | admission 29 euros online incl. audioguide, without having to queue. Outside high season, a limited number of tickets are available online for 15 euros (no audioguide) | start of tour: Place Denfert-Rochereau | M 4, 6, RER B Denfert-Rochereau | catacombes. paris.fr | ⊙ 45 mins | 14th arr. | ◻ K12*

51 MONTPARNASSE

The *Tour Montparnasse (summer daily 9.30am–11.30pm, winter Sun–Thu 9.30am–10.30pm, Fri/Sat until 11pm | 20 euros, online 19 euros | tourmontparnasse56.com),* a skyscraper that towers above everything else, was full of asbestos and for a long time could only really be appreciated when standing on its viewing platform. In preparation for the 2024 Olympic Games, the skyscraper has been given a modern makeover. When you wander through this district, you will find ugly buildings constructed in the 1960s alongside idyllic, green courtyards and studios once used by great artists and still used for artistic purposes today. Renowned artists such as Pablo Picasso, Amedeo Modigliani, Marc Chagall and Henri Matisse worked in the *Chemin du Montparnasse* on the avenue du Maine after World War I. The places they frequented, namely *La Coupole*, *Closerie des Lilas*, *Le Dôme* and *La Rotonde*, are still favourite meeting places. Lenin and Leo Trotsky held political meetings in La Rotonde that were regularly interrupted by the police. Literary figures such as Samuel Beckett and Charles Baudelaire, and the literary couple Jean-Paul Sartre and Simone de Beauvoir, are buried at the *Cimetière du Montparnasse*. *M 4, 6, 12, 13 Montparnasse-Bienvenüe | M 6 Edgar Quine | 14th arr. | ⚏ J-K 10-12*

🔢 ÎLE AUX CYGNES

Not far from the Eiffel Tower, a staircase leads down from the *Pont de Bir-Hakeim* to an island around 10m wide and 1km long. But unlike the other two islands on the Seine in Paris, this one was created artificially in 1825. Had enough of the mad city traffic? This is the perfect place to take a break: while cars zoom past on the left and right banks of the Seine, the *Allée des Cygnes* runs the length of

The catacombs preserve the remains of past generations

the entire island, and is reserved for strollers and joggers. The benches are just crying out for you to take a break.

At the other end of the island, the Statue of Liberty watches over the passing ships. Yes, Paris too has its own version of the Statue of Liberty by French sculptor Auguste Bartholdi. And not just one! Find replicas of Lady Liberty in the *Musée d'Orsay* (see p. 47), the *Musée des Arts et Métiers* (arts-et-metiers.net), the *Jardin du Luxembourg* (see p. 44), and the tunnel at the *Pont d'Alma*, where Princess Diana died in 1997. No need to go all the way to New York to marvel at the symbol of freedom that France once gifted to the USA! The 11.5m-high model on Île aux Cygnes, a present from the US for France to mark the centenary of the

INSIDER TIP
Lady Liberty – times five

French Revolution in 1889, will save you a few hours of flying. *M 6 Bir-Hakeim, M 10 Charles Michels | 15th arr. | ▭ D–E 8–9*

53 MUSÉE MARMOTTAN

The painting that gave Impressionism its name, *Impression Soleil Levant*, hangs next to a hundred other master-pieces by Claude Monet (1840–1926) on the lower level of this opulent villa near the Bois de Boulogne. Precious biblical paintings as well as paintings from Monet's private collection (including works by Edgar Degas, Edouard Manet and Auguste Renoir) hang in the upper living area. A must for every lover of Impressionist art! *Tue–Sun 10am–6pm (Thu until 9pm) | admission 12 euros | 2 rue Louis Boilly | marmottan.fr | M 9 La Muette | ⏱ 1.5 hrs | 16th arr. | ▭ C8*

Cross the Pont de Bir-Hakeim to reach the Île aux Cygnes (Swan Island)

54 PALAIS DE TOKYO

Not a museum in the classic sense. Contemporary artists present their sometimes provocative and huge installations in temporary exhibitions in halls constructed for the 1937 World Exposition, right next to the Musée d'Art Moderne de la Ville de Paris (see right). Satiate your hunger in one of the museum's two trendy and relaxed restaurants. *Wed-Mon noon–midnight | admission 12 euros | 13 av. du Président Wilson | palaisdetokyo.com | M 9 Iéna | ⏲ 2 hrs | 16th arr. | 🗺 F7*

55 MUSÉE D'ART MODERNE DE LA VILLE DE PARIS 🐌

Among the exhibits of modern art (Fernand Léger, Robert Delaunay, Pablo Picasso, Georges Braque and Amedeo Modigliani), you can admire Raoul Dufy's *La Fée Électricité* and *La Danse* by Henri Matisse. *Tue–Sun 10am–6pm (Thu temporary exhibitions until 10pm) | free admission, but a donation of 5 euros to support the museum is appreciated, temporary exhibitions 5-12 euros | 11 av. du Président Wilson | mam.paris.fr | M 9 Iéna | ⏲ 2 hrs | 16th arr. | 🗺 F7*

56 LE CORBUSIER

Seventeen works by French-Swiss architect Le Corbusier were named World Heritage Sites in 2016. You can visit two of these buildings in Paris: the home of art collector Raoul La Roche and the studio and flat of the architect himself. Both buildings are about a 20-minute walk apart. *Studio & apartment (Thu/Fri 1.30–6.30pm, Sat 10am–1pm & 1.30-6pm, closed Aug | admission 10 euros, joint ticket 15 euros | 24 rue Nungesser et Coli | M 10 Porte d'Auteuil| 16th arr. | 🗺 B10). Maison La Roche (Tue, Thu–Sat 10am–6pm | 10 Square du Docteur Blanche | M 9 Jasmin | 16th arr. | 🗺 B9). Both: fondationlecorbusier.fr | ⏲ around 1 hr each.*

57 BOIS DE BOULOGNE

The large green lung to the west of Paris covering an area of over 8 sqkm was a fashionable recreational meeting place at the beginning of the 20th century. Many hiking, riding and bicycle trails, as well as small lakes, two horse-racing tracks and diverse restaurants are located in the park, but its forests have sadly been dissected by many roads and are now the workplace of prostitutes. In the 18th century, the nobility built small summer residences here. One of the most popular is the small castle of Bagatelle in the *Parc de Bagatelle (admission April–Sept 2.50 euros, Oct-March free)*, which is beautifully manicured and intersected by streams. The rose garden is a delight for flower lovers.

The nearby 🐒 *Jardin d'Acclimatation* is a children's paradise and an oasis in the big city also for grown-ups. There are two bicycle rental agencies and rowing boats for hire at the *Lac Inférieur. M 1 Les Sablons | 🗺 A–D 4–9*

58 FONDATION LOUIS VUITTON

A huge futuristic glass cloud designed by the famous architect Frank Gehry graces the eastern part of Bois de Boulogne. The building, with its

Fondation Louis Vuitton: even the building is an avant-garde work of art

slightly confusing galleries ranging in height from 11m to 21m, is a masterpiece in itself. It houses recent pieces by internationally renowned artists, including Gerhard Richter, Marina Abramović, Damien Hurst and Olafur Eliasson. Temporary exhibitions as well as contemporary music concerts round out the offerings. *Changing opening times depending on season & events | admission 14 euros | 8 av. du Mahatma Gandhi | fondationlouis vuitton.fr | M1 Le Sablons | ⏱ 2 hrs | ⩍ B5*

59 JARDIN D'ACCLIMATATION 👪

Nestled in the elegant part of the Bois de Boulogne, this place bears witness to the charm of the 19th century with unusual playgrounds, merry-go-rounds, animals and watercourses. *Mon–Fri 11am–6pm, Sat/Sun 10am–7pm | day ticket 35 euros including carousel rides | jardindacclimatation. fr | M 1 Les Sablons | ⏱ at least 1/2 day, best to spend a day | ⩍ B4–5*

MONT-MARTRE TO BELLEVILLE

Over in the north of the city, the 17th to 20th arrondissements stretch from west to east. North of the Place de Ternes and the Parc Monceau, the 17th arrondissement shows that it's a grandiose part of the city.

The sheer splendour of the 19th-century townhouses is unmistakeable in *rue Fortuny*, where Edmond Rostand wrote his *Cyrano de*

Bergerac and where former French President Nicolas Sarkozy grew up. To the north of the 17th, where people live much more modestly, a new eco-district, *Clichy-Batignolles*, has sprung up around the *Parc Martin Luther-King*.

The number 18, meanwhile, instantly brings to mind the legendary artists' and nightlife district of ★ *Montmartre* (see Discovery Tour 3, p. 135), which is of course a must-see. But if you want to delve deeper into multicultural Paris afterwards, don't hop straight back on the Métro right away. The 18th arrondissement has another side to it – less picturesque, but with no less of a buzz! On your way to the 19th, you'll pass through the African quarter of *Goutte d'Or*, considered a no-go area by some Parisians. But a whole range of creatives have called the neighbourhood

home and commemorate it in their work. Examples include fashion designer Sakina M'sa's "Goutte d'Or, j'adore" t-shirts and director Clément Cogitore's film *Goutte d'Or*, shown at the Cannes Film Festival in 2022.

Once you reach the 19th arrondissement, walk along the *Canal de l'Ourcq* to the *Parc de la Villette (lavillette.com)*. Where slaughterhouses stood as late as the 1970s, there is now a huge park with themed gardens, playgrounds, museums and event venues. Not much further is Napoleon III's *Parc des Buttes-Chaumont*, where Parisians love to laze out on the grass in the sun. Once you've had your fill of the slow life, finish up with the 20th and a stroll through fashionable *Belleville*, before paying your respects to Jim Morrison at the *Père Lachaise* cemetery.

🚇 LES BATIGNOLLES

There really is a Paris beyond the hordes of tourists! This is the perfect spot to take a leaf out of the book of everyday Parisians. Here, young but well-off families scramble for the flats around the church of *Sainte-Marie-des-Batignolles* opposite the Square des Batignolles. The *Marché des Batignolles (Tue–Sun | 96 bis, rue Lemercier)* is ideally placed to supply locals with fruit and vegetables. If organic produce is your thing, head to the *Marché biologique* (see p. 100) on Saturdays. Take your time and stroll along the rue des Batignolles and the rue Legendre as far as the rue Lemercier. It won't take long to see why the area held such a special place

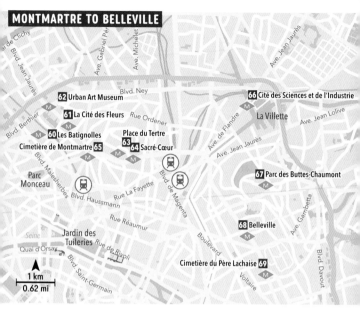

62 Urban Art Museum
66 Cité des Sciences et de l'Industrie
La Villette
61 La Cité des Fleurs
60 Les Batignolles
Place du Tertre
Cimetière de Montmartre 65
63 64 Sacré-Cœur
Parc Monceau
67 Parc des Buttes-Chaumont
Jardin des Tuileries
68 Belleville
Cimetière du Père Lachaise 69

1 km
0.62 mi

in the hearts of artists such as the painter Édouard Manet, the writer Émile Zola or the *chansonnier* Jacques Brel. *M 13 Brochant | ⏱ a relaxed 1/2 day | 17th arr. | 🗺 H–J3*

61 LA CITÉ DES FLEURS

Few Parisians are lucky enough to live in a villa with a verdant front garden.

INSIDER TIP
Stroll down a leafy lane

Fortunately, the residents of this 320m-long pedestrianised, private street are kind enough to open the gate to visitors at certain times. A memorial plaque here commemorates a sad piece of history: two resistance fighters were executed and a further six deported under Nazi occupation in house no. 25. That was 1944, just a few months after actress Catherine

Deneuve was born on this very street. *Mon–Sat 7am–7pm, Sun 7am–1pm | Cité des Fleurs | M 13 Brochant | 17th arr. | 🗺 H–J2*

62 URBAN ART MUSEUM (ART42)

OK, you probably wouldn't put the words "street art" and "museum" together right off the bat. But that is exactly what street art collector Nicolas Laugero Lasserre has done, settling on the innovative 42 computer coding school as the venue for this exhibition. Book in advance for a I free guided tour through this enclave of urban art – 150 works by 50 artists on 4000sq m to be precise. Genre classics kick things off on the ground floor of what is France's very first peer-to-peer university, with works by Shepard Fairey, Invader and JR. Up on the first floor, the tour continues with French street classics, while the last floor is dedicated to the rising stars on the scene. *Every second Tue 6–9pm, guided tour in English at 7pm | free admission | 96 bd. Bessières | art42.fr | M 13, 14, RER C Porte de Clichy | ⏱ 1.5 hrs | 17th arr. | ⮑ H1*

63 PLACE DU TERTRE

There is hardly a trace of the former village-like calm here. Instead, the area has been taken over by droves of tourists clamouring for their portrait to be rendered by artists of varying degrees of talent. The cafés that border the square are ideal for reminiscing about the era when luminaries of the arts still whiled away their time here. *M 12 Abesses | 18th arr. | ⮑ L3*

64 SACRÉ-CŒUR

The dazzling white basilica rising high above the city on the hill of Montmartre seems almost surreal, and cynics claim the domes look as if a confectioner has been having fun. The interior contains a stunning giant golden Byzantine-style mosaic. The edifice was built as a national monument after France's defeat by Germany in the Franco-Prussian War of 1870/71. In 1919 the pilgrimage church was dedicated to the Sacred Heart of Jesus. Today, thousands make the pilgrimage up the many steps and enjoy the impressive view over Paris from the church's forecourt. A more comfortable option for making the ascent is a small mountain railway (price: one metro ticket or free with a day ticket).

Daily 6.30am–10.30pm | 35 rue du Chevalier de la Barre | sacre-coeur-montmartre.com | M 2 Anvers | 18th arr. | ⮑ L3

65 CIMETIÈRE DE MONTMARTRE

A number of artists and literati including Hector Berlioz, Heinrich Heine, Alexandre Dumas, Edgar Degas, Jacques Offenbach, François Truffaut, Vaslav Nijinsky, Emile Zola and Stendhal found their final resting place in this picturesque cemetery. *Daily 8/9am–5.30/6pm | 20 av. Rachel (main entrance) | M 2 Blanche, M 2, 13 Place de Clichy | 18th arr. | ⮑ J–K3*

Portrait artists at work on the Place du Tertre

66 CITÉ DES SCIENCES ET DE L'INDUSTRIE 👺

This futuristic science museum transforms visitors into explorers with a submarine, flight simulator and planetarium. The attraction in the giant silver globe *La Géode (lageode.fr)* is a 360-degree cinema. *Tue–Sat 9.30am–6pm, Sun 9.30am–7pm | depending on selection, prices from 12 euros, children 9 euros | 30 av. Corentin Cariou | cite-sciences.fr | M 7 Porte de la Villette | 🕑 a relaxed 1/2 day | 19th arr. | 🕮 Q1–2*

67 PARC DES BUTTES-CHAUMONT

In the 19th century, Napoleon III had a picturesque landscaped park laid out in the English style with grottoes, rock formations, bridges, pavilions and waterfalls on a waste tip in the then-notorious eastern part of Paris. Today, it is just 15 minutes from the city centre. With the help of the most modern technology of the day and numerous explosives, the terraced grounds were created to a variety of different designs – including one with a lake and an island – and planted with unusual vegetation. *Every day in summer 7am–10pm, 7am–8pm in winter | M 7b Buttes-Chaumont | 19th arr. | 🕮 P–Q 4–5*

68 BELLEVILLE

In contrast to the wealthy west of the

A fantastical memorial at Pere Lachaise cemetery

SIGHTSEEING

city, the Belleville district has largely maintained its folksy charm. *Villa de l'Ermitage* and *Cité Leroy*, hidden alleyways lined with tiny houses, give us an idea of how 19th-century Parisian workers must have lived. You can still experience authentic local culture without all the tourist hype at a number of "*musette* bars" in the area – almost like back in the days when Edith Piaf was growing up here. Ever since artists discovered the charm and relatively low prices of the area, Belleville has become fashionable. Enjoy a beautiful view over Paris from the belvedere above Belleville Park, with alleyways winding up to it. *M 2, 11 Belleville | 20th arr. | ⬚ P–Q 5–6*

69 CIMETIÈRE DU PÈRE LACHAISE

With an area of 44 hectares, 12,000 trees, and 1.5 million graves including many ostentatious monuments, this cemetery is certainly the largest and most spectacular in Paris. In particular, the graves of Doors lead singer Jim Morrison and Edith Piaf attract huge numbers of visitors. Yves Montand with Simone Signoret, Maria Callas, Honoré de Balzac, Marcel Proust, Oscar Wilde, Frédéric Chopin and Molière are also buried here. *Daily 8/9am–5.30/6pm | main entrance: bd. Ménilmontant | pere lachaise.com | M 2, 3 Père Lachaise, M 2 Philippe Auguste | 20th arr. | ⬚ Q–R 7–8*

DAY TRIPS

70 DISNEYLAND PARIS 👯

40km/45 mins east from Châtelet-Les Halles (RER A bis Marne-la-Vallée - Chessy)

In the first 30 years since it opened in 1992, 375 million visitors have been to Walt Disney's fairytale dreamland, making it Europe's most popular tourist attraction. *Daily, see website for opening hours | day pass depending on season 56–105 euros, children 52–97 euros | 77700 Chessy | disney landparis.fr | ⏱ at least a day | ⬚ 0*

71 PARC ASTÉRIX 👯

40km/1 hr north-east from the city centre via the A 1, exit: Parc Astérix

A good French alternative to Disneyland, but a bit smaller. Asterix and his friends captivate visitors with all sorts of fun rides and a replica of the small village of the indomitable Gauls. *April–Dec (partly closed during the week outside school holidays) daily 10am–6pm, sometimes 10pm | admission 55 euros, 3–11s 47 euros, early-bird tariffs available online | 60128 Plailly | several bus companies offer trips from Paris | parcasterix.fr |* ⏱ *1 day* | 🗺 *0*

72 SAINT-DENIS

10km/20 mins north from Gare Saint-Lazare (M 13 to Basilique de Saint-Denis)

Stunning, early Gothic pillared basilica (begun in 1135) which became the prototype for this architectural style in France. A visit to the *royal tombs* is one of the highlights of any tour of this church, located in the Paris suburb of Saint-Denis. For centuries, nearly every ruler of the nation was buried here. There are 75 monumental tombs in the crypt, each guarded by life-sized statues of the deceased. The first church was built on this site in the fifth century after the martyr Denis allegedly walked up Montmartre with his severed head tucked under his arm in the year 250. *Summer Mon–Sat 10am–6.15pm, Sun noon–6.15pm, winter Mon–Sat 10am–5.15pm, Sun noon–5.15pm | tombs: 9.50 euros, free Nov–March and 1st Sun of the month | 1 rue de la Légion d'Honneur, Saint-Denis | saint-denis-basilique.fr |* 🗺 *0*

The pillars in the choir of Saint-Denis cathedral seem to stretch up to the heavens

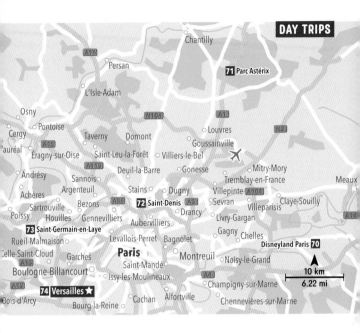

DAY TRIPS

73 SAINT-GERMAIN-EN-LAYE

20 km/25 mins west from Charles de Gaulle-Étoile (RER A to Saint-Germain-en-Laye)

Excursions to the old royal city Saint-Germain-en-Laye were already popular among Parisians in the 19th century. This was not only on account of the convenient connection by the nation's first railway system, constructed in 1837. French royalty had resided in the town of 40,000 inhabitants until the end of the 17th century. The landscape architects of Versailles laid out a beautiful *park* around the fortress-like, pentagonal *palace* with 2km-long viewing platform, high above the Seine. Saint-Germain has retained the flair of a pleasant provincial town. The old town's streets and pedestrianised lanes, with the beautiful palaces of the nobility, are ideal for a stroll and make an unforgettable outing. In addition, many shops are open on Sunday morning.

All this, and the large Saint-Germain forest, make for a truly unforgettable visit. In town, you can visit the *house where composer Claude Debussy was born (Wed–Fri 2–6pm, Sat 3–7pm, Sun 3–6pm | admission 5 euros, free 1st Sun of the month | 38 rue au Pain)*. The building is undergoing renovations until late 2023. The *studio of the Symbolist painter Maurice Denis (museemauricedenis.fr)*, with works by Paul Gauguin and Pierre Bonnard also on display, is worth a visit. *seine-saintgermain.fr* | 🕮 0

74 VERSAILLES ★

22 km/40 mins south-west from Saint-Michel Notre-Dame (RER C to Versailles-Rive Gauche)

A Paris stay is not complete without a visit to Louis XIV's gigantic palace. There is virtually nowhere else where the power of the monarch is displayed with such consistency and resoluteness, yet with such style and harmonious design, as in Versailles. The absolutist and centralist concept of a nation was personified by the "Sun King", Louis XIV (1638–1715). At his behest, nearly all of France's nobility resided here, which meant that as many as 20,000 people had to be provided for and entertained lavishly.

Absolute must-sees during the tour of the *palace (April–Oct Tue–Sun 9am–6.30pm, Nov–March Tue–Sun 9am–5.30pm | admission 18 euros, Nov–March 1st Sun of the month free)* are the *royal chapel*, the *opéra* and the *state rooms* on the first floor, the walls of which are finished in marble and decorated with gold brocade. Don't miss the 75m-long *Hall of Mirrors*, whose 17 windows cast light onto the mirrors opposite.

Once measuring 60km sq, the *park (April–Oct daily 8am–8.30pm, Nov–March daily 8am–6pm | admission free, except in summer for the Grandes Eaux Musicales 10 and 10.50 euros)* still covers an area of 800 hectares. During the *Grandes Eaux Musicales* classical music provides the background for water displays in the park's fountains.

In addition to the lake, where you can enjoy boat rides, other highlights include two smaller palaces, the *Grand* and *Petit Trianon*. The newly renovated *Domaine de Trianon (April–Oct Tue–Sun noon–6.30pm, Nov–March Tue–Sun noon–5.30pm | admission 12 euros)* includes grottoes, a temple of love and streams in the pretty English garden, as well as *Le Hameau*, an idealised replica of a village farm complete with pond. If you prefer not to walk, you can cycle or take a mini-train.

Complete Passport Château Versailles package *20 euros, 27 euros on days of Grandes Eaux Musicales and Jardins Musicaux.* Advance ticket sales online at *chateauversailles.fr.*

The easiest way to reach Versailles from Paris is on the suburban train RER C (Versailles-Rive Gauche), which takes around 30 minutes. The palace is only a short walk from the railway station. Trains to Versailles-Rive Droite (then bus) travel every 15 minutes from the Gare Saint-Lazare and from the Gare Montparnasse (direction Chartres) to Versailles-Chantier (then bus). Bus route 171 goes from the Métro station Pont de Sèvres (M 9) to the palace.

INSIDER TIP
There and back please!

When buying your ticket, it's best to get one for your return journey too. That way, you won't have to waste time with tedious queueing in Versailles. ⏲ *at least 1 day – wear comfortable footwear!* | 🔲 *0*

Versailles is France's most famous palace and a UNESCO World Heritage Site

EATING & DRINKING

Paris has many top-notch restaurants, as well as popular bistros and brasseries, but if you really want to discover the multi-faceted gastronomy of France for yourself, you need to know the fundamental aspects of French eating habits. To the French, a meal is also an essential means of social interaction and a vital ingredient in enhancing the quality of life.

Breakfast *(petit déjeuner)* in France is modest by the standards of many other nations, although brunch culture is on the rise.

You'll find all the venues in this chapter on the pull-out map 📖

Famous and much-loved Brasserie Bofinger

Traditionally, you'll need room for a much more substantial lunch *(déjeuner)*. It often lasts far longer than, but is only half the price of, dinner *(diner)*.

Most restaurants do not open for dinner until 8pm in the evening. The French like to start their evening with an *apéritif* (kir, champagne or pastis, or simply a beer), accompanied by more or less sophisticated nibbles. You'll then be faced with the decision whether to order *à la carte* (from the menu) or *table d'hôte* (a set meal).

WHERE TO EAT IN PARIS

RUE DU FAUBOUR POISSONNIÈRE A RUE DE PARADIS

The best spots for veggies and vegans

Boulevard Haussmann

Arrondissement de l'Élysée

Avenue des Champs-Élysées

RUE SAINTE-ANNE

Tokyo in Paris

Pyramides

Jardin des Tuileries

Jardins du Trocadéro

Les Ombres ★

BEAUPASSAGE

Gourmets flock to this pedestrian zone

Rue du Bac

Quai Voltaire

Arrondissement de Vaugirard

Boulevard Raspail

Jardin du Luxembourg

La Coupole ★

Vavin

RUE DU MONTPARNASSE

Paradise for crêpe connoisseurs

Arrondissement de l'Observatoire

Boulevard Brune

MARCO POLO HIGHLIGHTS

★ **BOUILLON JULIEN**
Paris's most splendidly decorated brasserie ➤ p. 74

★ **LA COUPOLE**
Art Deco temple with an artistic tradition ➤ p. 74

★ **HOLYBELLY 5**
Revolutionising the Paris brunch scene ➤ p. 78

★ **LES OMBRES**
Contemporary restaurant with a view of the Eiffel Tower ➤ p. 78

★ **SEPTIME**
Starred cuisine in an informal setting ➤ p. 79

★ **LE TRAIN BLEU**
Majestic *fin-de-siècle* decor – a feast for the senses ➤ p. 79

★ **L'ESCARGOT MONTORGUEIL**
Upscale traditional restaurant in a 19th-century building ➤ p. 79

PASSAGE BRADY
Little India

Parc des Buttes-Chaumont

Poissonnière

Arrondissement de l'Entrepôt

Château d'Eau

Bouillon Julien ★

Holybelly 5 ★

RUE MONTORGUEIL
Gastronomy mile that will fulfil your foodie dreams

Rue de la République

L'Escargot Montorgueil ★

Châtelet · Les Halles

Arrondissement du Temple

Rue de Rivoli

Arrondissement de Popincourt

Saint-Paul

Septime ★

Île Saint-Louis

RUE DES ROSIERS
Falafel sandwiches to die for

Arrondissement du Panthéon

Le Train Bleu ★

Jardin des Plantes

Arrondissement de Reuilly

Quai de Bercy

Arrondissement des Gobelins

CHINATOWN
must-visit for lovers of Asian cuisine

Olympiades

Rue de Tolbiac

1 km
0.62 mi

A set meal is better value for money if you are hungry, since it traditionally consists of an appetiser *(entrée)*, main course *(plat)* – usually meat *(viande)* or fish *(poisson)*, cheese *(fromage)* and/or dessert. Tap water *(eau en carafe)* and bread *(pain)* are automatically provided with your meal. A *café* or *déca* (decaffeinated coffee) at the end of your meal should not be forgotten. An extensive wine list is the sign of a good restaurant. A tip *(pourboire)* of 5–10 per cent is *de rigueur*.

BRASSERIES

Brasseries are very much part of the Paris scene. As opposed to small, cosy bistros with modest menus, brasseries are fairly large, informal restaurants, which sprang up at the turn of the 20th century and serve hearty fare in addition to seafood specialities. Many brasseries are in protected buildings with glamorous Belle-Époque decor. Though the food is not exactly cheap in these restaurants, it is still relatively affordable *(€€)*.

1 BOFINGER 🚩

The *choucroute de la mer* – sauerkraut with fish and other seafood – is a hit here, served in a striking Art Nouveau setting under a glass dome. *Daily | 5–7 rue de la Bastille | tel. 01 42 72 87 82 | bofingerparis.com | M 1, 5, 8 Bastille | 4th arr. | ▥ O8*

2 BRASSERIE LIPP 🚩

Probably the most famous brasserie in Paris. Here, you'll find statesmen, writers, actors and, of course, hordes of tourists. The food is anything but light. The restaurant's specialities: pork sausage with *remoulade*, and stuffed pig's trotters. The menu is extensive and there are rotating daily specials. *Daily | 151 bd. Saint-Germain-des-Prés | tel. 01 45 48 53 91 | brasserielipp.fr | M 4 Saint-Germain-des-Prés | 6th arr. | ▥ K8*

3 BOUILLON JULIEN ⭐

Extravagant stucco, vine-covered Art Nouveau maidens, colourful glass ceilings and mirrored walls. You couldn't be blamed for thinking you're in the last century, when clerks, students and workers from the north-east of Paris flocked here to eat. This brasserie has just been reopened under the motto of that time: "*beau, bon, pas cher*" (beautiful, good, reasonable). The house beef soup is just 9.90 euros! *Daily | 16, rue du Faubourg Saint-Denis | tel. 01 47 70 12 06 | julienparis.com | M 4, 8, 9 Strasbourg-Saint-Denis | 10th arr. | ▥ M6*

4 LA COUPOLE ⭐

In the 1920s, artists such as Chagall, Picasso and Dalí kept company in this Art Deco temple. The lamb curry is legendary; they've been making it here according to a traditional South Indian recipe since 1927. *Daily | 102 bd. du Montparnasse | tel. 01 43 20 14 20 | lacoupole-paris.com | M 4 Vavin | 14th arr. | ▥ J10*

5 LE CAFÉ DU COMMERCE

A little off the beaten track but still near enough to the Eiffel Tower, this establishment is happily located in a middle-class residential area and is proudly noisy and convivial over three open floors. The onion soup always goes down well as a starter. Feeling brave? Try the pork: everything from ears to trotters is served here. *Daily | 51 rue du Commerce | tel. 01 45 75 03 27 | lecafeducommerce.com | M 10 Avenue Émile Zola | 15th arr. | ▥ F10*

CAFÉS

Paris is famous for its cafés. Among the storied, classic cafés that live up to their historic reputation are the *Café de Flore* and the *Les deux Magots*. If you want to experience today's authentic Paris, the best place to go is any café in a residential district that doesn't attract many tourists. You'll meet real Parisians here, and the 🐖 coffee will be much cheaper! Drinking your coffee at the bar is often less expensive, and you're more likely to fall into conversation with the regulars.

INSIDER TIP
Stand and save money

⑥ LES DEUX MAGOTS

This famous *café littéraire* (according to its own publicity), where Ernest Hemingway came to drink whiskey, is named after the two Chinese porcelain figures at the entrance. It is a treat to sit on the terrace facing Saint-Germain-des-Prés church. *Daily | 6 pl. Saint-Germain-des-Prés | tel. 01 45 48 55 25 | lesdeuxmagots.fr | M 4 Saint-Germain-des-Prés | 6th arr. | ▥ K8*

Artists and writers have long enjoyed dining in La Coupole's art deco surroundings

Café de Flore was once a meeting place for existentialists; now it's a tourist hotspot

7 CAFÉ DE FLORE

An institution and meeting place for artists, literary figures and intellectuals since Simone de Beauvoir, Jean-Paul Sartre and Albert Camus were regulars here. Today, it is a place to see and be seen, whether for fashionistas or tourists. *Daily | 172 bd. Saint-Germain | tel. 01 45 48 55 26 | cafedeflore.fr | M 4 Saint-Germain-des-Prés | 6th arr. | 🗺 K8*

8 LE BARBOUQUIN

Invitingly colourful and unconventional, and a beloved hub of 21st-century literary Paris. This "book bar" is a bookshop, meeting spot for artists, and café all in one, located in the Belleville district, a hot spot for street artists. Regular literary events are held here, as are unannounced theatre performances. *Closed Tue | 1 rue Denoyez | tel. 09 84 32 13 21 | facebook.com/lebarbouquin | M 2, 11 Belleville | 20th arr. | 🗺 P6*

BRUNCH

9 CAFÉ JOZI

Word travels fast on the Seine when the food is good, so you may face a long queue, especially at weekends. As they don't accept bookings, your best bet is to stop by during the week to try their delicious pancakes with fresh fruit. *Brunch daily 8am–3pm | 3 rue Valette | tel. 06 12 32 02 67 | Facebook: Jozi Café | M 10 Cardinal Lemoine | 5th arr. | 🗺 L9*

Today's specials

Entrées

SOUPE À L'OIGNON GRATINÉE
Onion soup topped with melted cheese

BOUILLABAISSE
Soupy stew made with Mediterranean fish and seafood

ESCARGOTS À LA BOURGUIGNONNE
Snails served in their shells with a garlicky sauce

Viandes (Meat)

BŒUF BOURGUIGNON
Beef stew braised in red wine

COQ AU VIN
Chicken stew braised in red wine

NOISETTES D'AGNEAU
Small lamb cutlets fried in butter

CÔTES DE PORC AUX HERBES
Pork chops with herbs

Poissons (Fish)

PLATEAU DE FRUITS DE MER
Seafood platter, usually with *crevettes* (prawns), *crabe* (crab), *moules* (mussels), *huîtres* (oysters) – often served raw

MOULES MARINIÈRES
Mussels steamed in white wine and garlic

BROCHETTES DE COQUILLES
Scallop kebabs

AILE DE RAIE AU BEURRE
Skate wings fried in butter

Desserts

TARTE TATIN
Caramelised upside-down apple tart

CRÈME BRÛLÉE
Dessert made from egg yolk, sugar, cream, milk and vanilla

PROFITEROLES
Small rounds of choux pastry filled with whipped cream or custard, topped with chocolate sauce

Drinks

GRENADINE
Still water with grenadine syrup

DIABOLO MENTHE
Lemonade with peppermint syrup

KIR
White wine with *crème de cassis* or another fruit liqueur

10 EGGS & CO

The name says it all! If you fancy eggs, free-range of course, this is your spot. They're prepared in every imaginable way: the classic French option is *œufs cocottes*, eggs from the oven, served with potatoes and salad – delicious! The ambience is a little cramped but very cosy… Think of it as like a chicken coop! *Closed Wed | 11 rue Bernard-Palissy | tel. 01 45 44 02 52 | eggsandco.fr | M 4 Saint-Germain-des-Prés | 6th arr. | K9*

11 HOLYBELLY 5 ★

Sarah Mouchot and Nico Alary have been together since high school. Before the young couple revolutionised the Paris brunch scene by opening Holybelly, the French natives lived and worked for a while in Canada and Australia – hence the Anglo-Saxon touch. The speciality here is the pancakes topped with bacon and maple syrup. And they are overrun with business! No wonder: breakfast served from 9am to 5pm is not an option across the board in Paris. The queue was getting so long on Saturdays and Sundays that Holybelly now uses the app Skeepit on weekends to keep things in order. *Daily until 5pm, last orders 4pm | 5 rue Lucien Sampaix | tel. 01 82 28 00 80 | holybellycafe.com | M 5 Jacques Bonsergent | 10th arr. | N6*

INSIDER TIP
Breakfast all day

RESTAURANTS €€€

12 MYSTERY CUISINE

The name says it all! Vietnamese Thu Ha and her French husband Edouard conjure up molecular dishes that will transport you to new galaxies of taste – but the menu won't reveal what's on your plate. This restaurant is full of surprises – both culinary and atmospheric. There are just three tables, so be sure to make a reservation! *Closed Sun/Mon & lunchtime | 37 bis, rue de Montpensier | tel. 01 40 20 03 02 | mysterycuisine.fr | M 8, 14 Pyramides | 1st arr. | K6*

13 BEL CANTO

Looking for somewhere a bit special? A unique restaurant in which trained opera singers, accompanied by a piano, belt out arias by Verdi, Puccini and others as you enjoy the fine Italian cuisine. A sophisticated dining experience based on the motto *"les diners lyriques". Closed Sun/Mon & lunch | 72 quai de l'Hôtel de Ville | tel. 01 42 78 30 18 | lebelcanto.com | M 1, 11 Hôtel de Ville | 4th arr. | M8*

14 LES OMBRES ★

You will not find a more spectacular view of the Eiffel Tower than through the glass roof of this restaurant at the Musée du Quai Branly – Jacques Chirac. In the summer you can enjoy the imaginatively prepared meals – variations of French classics – and the exquisite atmosphere from the terrace. *Closed Sun/Mon | 27 quai Branly | tel. 01 47 53 68 00 | lesombres-restaurant.com | M 9 Iéna | 7th arr. | F7*

15 SEPTIME ★

This restaurant dishes up star cuisine from young talent. Top chef Bertrand Grébaut was a graffiti artist in a former life, and his restaurant in the hip north-east of Paris is correspondingly chill. While Michelin-starred, Septime is anti-elitist, and the five- to seven-course menu is as simple as the decor. But since stars like Beyoncé and Jay-Z have been spotted eating here, the tables are often booked up to three weeks in advance. *Closed Sat/Sun | 80 rue de Charonne | tel. 01 43 67 38 29 | septime-charonne.fr | M 9 Charonne | 11th arr. | ⃞ P8*

16 LE TRAIN BLEU ★ 🍸

Without a doubt the most exquisite station restaurant in the world. The 6m-high ceilings are reminiscent of a dining hall at Versailles. Should you find the prices for the classic French cuisine too prohibitive, opt for a cocktail instead of the house speciality of grilled leg of lamb with potato gratin, and enjoy the glorious atmosphere in one of the comfortable leather armchairs in the bar. *Daily | pl. Louis Armand | tel. 01 43 43 09 06 | le-train-bleu.com | M 1, 14, RER A, D Gare de Lyon | le-train-bleu.com | 12th arr. | ⃞ O-P10*

RESTAURANTS €€

17 L'ESCARGOT MONTORGUEIL ★

A traditional restaurant established in 1832, decorated in classic late Empire style. Luminaries such as Marcel Proust, Charlie Chaplin, Pablo Picasso and Jacqueline Kennedy have dined

Fortunately, "snail's pace" doesn't describe the service

here. The name *escargot* – snail – says it all. You can sample numerous different variations of the molluscs here. Snails with parsley and garlic butter are especially popular, while snails with foie gras or black truffles are a posh treat. You can even try exotic curry snails! But don't worry: You don't *have* to eat snails. The upscale menu has something for everyone – even vegetarians. *Daily | 38 rue Montorgueil | tel. 01 42 36 83 51 | escargotmontorgueil.com | M 4 Etienne Marcel | 1st arr. | ⃞ L7*

18 MACEO

Innovative, contemporary restaurant with a large, light and comfortable dining area. Also serves one or two vegetarian dishes. A small library and bar entice you to linger a little longer. *Closed Sat lunch & Sun | 15 rue des Petits-Champs | tel. 01 42 97 53 85 | M 3 Bourse | maceorestaurant. com | 1st arr. | ▯ L6*

19 AU VIEUX PARIS

Located next to Notre-Dame, this is where the canons lived back in 1512. Traditional French cuisine has been served here since 1750! The exuberantly plush furnishings with a Gothic touch create a romantic atmosphere; the set meal is substantial and not expensive by Parisian standards. *Daily | 24 rue Chanoinesse | tel. 01 40 51 78 52 | restaurantauvieuxparis. fr | M 4 Cité | 4th arr. | ▯ M8*

20 LE JARDIN DES PÂTES 👯

Right next door to the Jardin des Plantes is the "pasta garden". It's the perfect stop if you're leaving the Natural History Museum with hungry kids and a real Latin Quarter institution! Since 1984, the chefs here have made fresh pasta from all sorts of different types of grain – all organic. A house classic is the chestnut pasta with duck breast fillet, nutmeg, crème fraîche and mushrooms. To die for! *Daily | 4 rue Lacépède | tel. 01 43 31 50 71 | M 7 Place Monge | 5th arr. | ▯ M10*

INSIDER TIP
Feast in pasta paradise

Purple flowering wisteria adorns the entrance and courtyard of Au Vieux Paris

21 ALCAZAR

A trendy hotspot for jetsetters, with a glass roof and lots of greenery. The restaurant is very French, with snails and frogs' legs on the menu. The bar upstairs also offers small but delicious bites – so the cocktails won't knock you out! DJ from Wednesday to Saturday from 10 pm. *Closed Sun/Mon | 62 rue Mazarine | tel. 01 53 10 19 99 | alcazar. fr | M 4, 10 Odéon | 6th arr. | ☐ K8*

22 BOUILLON RACINE

Decorative Art Nouveau ornamentation in a pleasing shade of spring green winds around two storeys of windows, mirrors and wood at Bouillon Racine. Even the mosaic floor has been meticulously restored in this former workers' cafeteria. The traditional French cuisine includes snails, foie gras and duck breast. *Daily | 3 rue Racine | tel. 01 44 32 15 60 | bouillon-racine.com | M 10, RER B Cluny-La Sorbonne | 6th arr. | ☐ L9*

23 CALIFE

"Paris, the city of love." Some clichés exist for a reason, and this two-hour cruise (at noon and in the evening) along the islands of the Seine might be one of those reasons. With a three-course menu (from 97 euros including boat ticket), the organisers hope to prove that Paris has earned its moniker. Make sure to reserve tickets early! *Closed Tue | Quai Malaquais, near Pont des Arts | tel. 01 43 54 50 04 | calife.com | M 1 Louvre-Rivoli | 6th arr. | ☐ K8*

24 LE P'TIT TROQUET

Tiny bistro with authentic 1920s flair, cordially serving sophisticated and refined traditional French cuisine such as "house rabbit terrine with pistachios, pickled carrots and red onions". It's good value for money, especially considering its close proximity to the Eiffel Tower. *Closed Sat & Mon lunch, all Sun | 28 rue de l'Exposition | tel. 01 85 15 24 64 | leptittroquet.fr | M8 Ecole Militaire | 7th arr. | ☐ G8*

25 POLMARD

Right at the heart of gourmet territory in *Beaupassage* passage, Polmard, the traditional butcher from Lorraine and supplier to the great star chefs, has now opened its first Parisian restaurant. Alexandre Polmard has been running his family farm since 2013 and serves the very best beef from his legendary Blondes d'Aquitaine. *Closed Sun/Mon & Tue lunch | 53–57 rue de Grenelle | tel. 01 43 21 30 30 | polmard.com | M 12 rue du Bac | 7th arr. | ☐ J8*

26 LE PETIT PÉKIN

Local residents come back to Zhao, who is from Beijing, time and time again. The menu is short, but only because the traditional Chinese cuisine is cooked here with fresh ingredients – which goes down well with the regulars. Just a heads-up: the ravioli are addictive. *Closed Sun | 162 av. Parmentier | tel. 09 50 59 95 34 | M 11 Goncourt | 10th arr. | ☐ O6*

27 SOYA

Vegetarian/vegan restaurant near the Canal Saint-Martin that's 100 per cent organic, in a light, airy loft-like space with parquet floors, wooden tables and an open kitchen. Christel Dhuit and her team now serve fusion food in this former plumbers' workshop. At weekends, hip Parisians come here for a hearty, healthy brunch after a night of drinking and partying. *Daily | 20 rue de la Pierre Levée | tel. 01 85 15 28 02 | soya-cantine-bio. fr | M 11 Goncourt | 11th arr. | ⊞ O6*

INSIDER TIP
Great vegetarian brunch

28 LE SAUT DU CAPRAUT

This restaurant from former Mexican banker Marco Paz serves French cuisine with a Mexican twist. A personal food love story from an honorary Parisian that you won't regret sampling. *Closed Sun dinner & Mon lunch | 16 rue des Plantes | tel. 01 40 44 73 09 | lesautducrapaud.zenchef. com | M 4 Mouton-Duvernet | 14th arr. | ⊞ J12*

RESTAURANTS €

29 BISTROT RICHELIEU

The comfortable atmosphere in this restaurant is exactly what you need after an exhausting visit to the neighbouring Louvre. Typical French dishes such as snails, onion soup and duck grace the tables. *Closed Sun | 45 rue de Richelieu | tel. 01 42 60 19 16 | bistrotrichelieu.com | M 1, 7 Palais Royal – Musée du Louvre | 1st arr. | ⊞ K6*

30 LE MESTURET

Although it's been a few years since it won the award for Bistro of the Year, this locale has maintained its high standards of quality. In the mood for a veal stew just like grandma would make, a classic steak tartare or a duck burger? Then this is the place for you! *Closed Sat lunch, Sun | 77, rue de Richelieu | tel. 01 42 97 40 68 | lemesturet.com | M 3 Bourse | 2nd arr. | ⊞ L6*

31 MÛRE

The concept is simple: fruit and veg are grown on an organic farm not far from Paris before the harvest is processed in this small, hip restaurant and dished up to hungry city dwellers for breakfast, lunch or coffee. And since the vast majority of ingredients come straight from field to plate, you don't have to cough up for transport or middlemen. That means you can enjoy the healthy and tasty lunch menu here for just over 10 euros. The only problem: the crowds! After all, sustainability is all the rage in Paris right now. *Mon–Fri 8.30am–3.30pm, Sat 11am–5pm | 6 rue Saint Marc | mure-restaurant.com | M 8, 9 Grands Boulevards | 2nd arr. | ⊞ L6*

INSIDER TIP
Totally local

32 CHEZ MARIANNE

This busy restaurant with a terrace and a delicatessen is located around the corner from the lively rue des Rosiers at the centre of the Marais district. Try the popular Middle Eastern appetiser platter. *Daily | 2 rue des Hospitalières*

Study the menu options at Chez Marianne before you choose

Saint-Gervais | tel. 01 42 72 18 86 | *chezmarianne.fr* | M 1 Saint-Paul | *4th arr.* | ☐ N8

33 LA FOURMI AILÉE

The atmosphere in the "winged ant", not far from Notre-Dame, is relaxed and cosy. The loaded bookshelves lining the walls bear witness to a time when books were still sold here. Today, you can dine on quiches, salads, traditional meat dishes, and vegetarian meals in this historic location. It's also the perfect place to stop for a cup of tea or espresso while you're on the go. *Daily | 8 rue du Fouarre | tel. 0143 29 40 99 | parisresto.com | M 10 Cluny-La Sorbonne | 5th arr.* | ☐ M9

34 LES PAPILLES

The perfect detour after a stroll in the Jardin du Luxembourg. The daily changing "back from the market" menu features regional products prepared as simple dishes. If you enjoy your meal, you can pop into the deli afterwards and load up your bags with goodies. *Closed Sun/Mon | 30 rue Gay Lussac | tel. 01 43 25 20 79 | les papillesparis.fr | RER B Luxembourg | 5th arr.* | ☐ L10

35 CAFÉ A

Only insiders are aware of the hip meeting spot for artists – including a café, bar and restaurant – behind the walls of this former monastery next to the Gare de l'Est. It's particularly recommended in good weather – then you can eat under the

> **INSIDER TIP**
> Artists'
> garden
> meeting place

trees of the monastery garden. The menu changes with the seasons. Wide selection of organic wines. *Tue–Sat until 2am, Sun/Mon until 5pm | 148 rue du Faubourg Saint-Martin | tel. 07 71 61 10 38 | cafea.fr | M 4, 5, 7 Gare de l'Est | 10th arr. | ⌐ N5*

36 URFA DÜRÜM

It's small, but it will surprise you: Urfa Dürüm makes the city's best Kurdish sandwiches! The pitta bread is prepared right in front of you and filled with fresh ingredients. When the crowds get too big, the cooks whip out a hairdryer and get up the fire under the grill going more strongly. You sit on low wooden stools. If that sounds uncomfortable, you can take your food

---

HOUSE BLEND

France is rediscovering coffee thanks to the growing popularity of coffee shops that roast their own beans among young Parisians. Courses and tastings akin to wine seminars are even offered at *Caféotheque (52 rue de l'Hôtel de Ville | www.lacafeotheque.com | 4th arr. | ⌐ M8).* The coffee is also freshly roasted at *Café Lomi (3 rue Marcadet | lomi.coffee | 18th arr. | ⌐ M2).* Snacks such as banana bread and select cheeses are the perfect accompaniment to these new *grand crus.* Stylish café *Coutume (47 rue de Babylone | coutumecafe.com | 7th arr. | ⌐ H9)* also stocks a huge selection of coffees.

---

and stroll over to the nearby Canal Saint-Martin. *Daily | two branches: 10 & 58, rue du Faubourg Saint-Denis | tel. 01 48 24 12 84 | FB: Urfa Durum | M 4 Château d'Eau | 10th arr. | ⌐ M5*

37 AUJOURD'HUI DEMAIN

Vegan restaurant with a concept store. The place to be for the city's vegans – and others. Not vegan, but utterly irresistible and at least vegetarian, is the red fruit cheesecake. Even omnivores will be convinced! *Daily | 42 rue du Chemin Vert | tel. 09 81 65 20 01 | aujourdhui-demain.com | M 8 Richard Lenoir | 11th arr. | ⌐ O–P8*

38 LE FOODMARKET 🐖

Young French globetrotter Virginie Godard has shown Parisians that street food can be cheap and delicious: her Food Market is a huge success. It's a culinary trip from kebabs to starred cuisine and you never pay more than 10 euros for a dish. Mothers, hipsters and businessmen alike come together here to enjoy a good meal. *1 Thu per month 6pm–10.30pm | bd. de Belleville between Couronnes & Ménilmontant métro stations | tel. 06 35 54 04 61 | lefoodmarket.fr | M2 Couronnes or Ménilmontant | 11th/20th arr. | ⌐ P5–6*

INSIDER TIP
Good food, low prices!

39 PAUSE CAFÉ

The "coffee break" is a cool restaurant in a cool quarter right behind the Bastille. Whether you're after a meal or just a cup of coffee or a glass on the terrace: if you like it young and stylish, then this is the address for you. Uncomplicated bistro cuisine. *Closed Sun | 41 rue de Charonne | tel. 01 48 06 80 33 | pausecafe.paris | M 1, 5, 8 Bastille | 11th arr. | ⌑ P9*

40 CHEZ GLANDINES

This restaurant on the Butte aux Cailles is where young, hungry Parisians go to eat hearty southwestern French meals on the cheap. And the restaurant doesn't take reservations: waiting outside with a glass of wine and good company is part of the experience. *Daily | 30 rue des Cinq Diamants | tel. 09 67 31 96 46 | chezgladines-butteauxcailles.fr | M 6 Corvisart | 13th arr. | ⌑ M12*

41 AUX ARTISTES 🐷

A loud and sociable spot. The name pays tribute to the time when artists like Amadeo Modigliani or Léonard Foujita expressed their creativity in this quarter. Now owned by the third generation of the same family since 1959, Marvin serves up down-to-earth French cuisine. For 16 euros, you get lunch or dinner including starter, main course and desert. So it is no huge surprise that the place is always full! *Closed Sat lunch, Sun | 63 rue Falguière | tel. 01 43 22 05 39 | auxartistes.fr | M 6, 12 Pasteur | 15th arr. | ⌑ H11*

House-roasted coffee, bread and just the right cheese: welcome to Café Lomi

Chat with friends and neighbours over a glass of red at Le Rubis

42 HOBA

The latest in place in the eco-district at Parc Martin Luther-King. The name is a play on the words *"haut"* (above) and *"bas"* (below): the upper area is a food court, while the historic lower building houses a café where events take place. The project presents itself as sustainable and forward-looking, experimenting with new, environmentally friendly approaches to gastronomy. *Daily | 147 rue Cardinet (access after park closes: 43, rue Bernard Buffet) | tel. 01 83 64 02 11 | hoba.paris | M 13, 14, RER C Porte de Clichy | 17th arr. | f H2*

43 LA RECYCLERIE

Hip vintage-style café/restaurant with an attached urban farm and repair workshop in a former train station near the Saint-Ouen flea market. The eatery serves sustainable cuisine with fresh ingredients and minimal meat. Thursdays are *"Jeudi veggie"*, when there is zero meat on the menu. Kitchen waste is fed directly to the chickens (yes, you can even find chickens in Paris!) or used as compost for the vegetable garden along the disused railway tracks. In good weather, you can sit outdoors. It's a little oasis of green, shielded from the bustle of the big city. *Open daily (Fri/Sat until 2am) | 83 bd. Ornano | tel. 01 42 57 58 49 | larecyclerie.com | M 4 Porte de Clignancourt | 18th arr. | ⊞ L1*

44 LE VIEUX BELLEVILLE 🐷

Alongside hearty French food, you can enjoy singalongs of French chansons – just as you've been able to do for 30 years. Don't know the lyrics? No problem! They hand out lyric sheets, and then it begins. On Tuesdays, Edith Piaf is on the programme. The brainchild of Joseph Pantaleo aka Jojo, who was born a few houses down the road over half a century ago, it's a popular place, so it's best to make reservations. *Closed Sun | singalong Tue, Thu–Sat 8pm–2am | 12 rue des Envierges | tel. 01 44 62 92 66 | le-vieux-belleville. com | M 11 Pyrénées | 20th arr. | ⌐ Q5*

WINE BARS

⁴⁵ LE RUBIS

The simple wine bar has remained virtually unchanged since its opening in 1948. Large wine selection, cheese platter and always a traditional daily special. *Closed Sun | 10 rue du Marché Saint-Honoré | tel. 01 42 61 03 34 | le-rubis-paris.fr | M 8, 14 Pyramides | 1st arr. | ⌐ K6*

⁴⁶ LEVAIN LE VIN

Sourdough *(levain)* and wine *(le vin)* – this place has in a small range of

high-quality produce. Christophe Fertillet specialises in selected wines and organic, quality home-baked bread. Then there is sausage, cheese and tapas – simple, but simply good! *Closed Sun/ Mon | 83 rue du Faubourg-Saint-Martin | tel. 01 42 45 49 10 | levainlevin.com | M 4 Château-d'Eau | 10th arr. | ⌐ N5*

INSIDER TIP
Simple and delicious

⁴⁷ LE BARON ROUGE

A small wine bar with a special flair. It's particularly lively in the Baron Rouge on Sunday at lunchtime, when, after shopping at the nearby Marché d'Aligre, the Parisians stand together around wine barrels in front of the bar enjoying a glass of wine and oysters. *Daily | 1 rue Théophile-Roussel | tel. 01 43 43 14 32 | lebaronrouge.net | M 8 Ledru-Rollin | 12th arr. | ⌐ P9*

VEGGIETOWN

The waiter looks absolutely baffled: "What do you mean, you don't eat meat?" Until quite recently, this would have been a likely scenario in a Paris restaurant, with few vegetarian options to be found. But vegetarianism is on the rise here now. There are growing numbers of hip restaurants with vegetarian or vegan menu items, especially in the trendy districts north of the Seine. Around *rue du Faubourg Poissonnière* and *rue de Paradis* (⌐ *L–M5*) on the border between the 9th and 10th arrondissements, the selection of vegetarian dining options is so enormous that the *Association végétarienne de France* (www.vegetarisme.fr) dubbed this area the "Veggietown" of Paris.

The bad old days when vegetarians had to settle for a boring salad at Parisian restaurants are a thing of the past!

SHOPPING

From haute couture to colourful food markets, shopping (or window shopping) in Paris is an experience: just wandering through the shopping streets has entertainment value. Paris offers the best of everything, and some visitors even make a special trip to take advantage of clearance sales (*soldes*) that occur twice a year (January and June/July), when you can bag discounts of up to 70 per cent.

Most shops are open from 10am to 7.30pm, Monday to Saturday. On Thursdays, large department stores have longer opening hours

You'll find all the venues in this chapter on the pull-out map 🗺

The luxurious Galeries Lafayette

known as *nocturne* (evening shopping). If you want to shop on Sunday, stores in the Marais, the lower ground floor at the Louvre and some shops on the Champs-Elysées are open all day. Department stores and many other shops are open on the last three or four Sundays before Christmas.

Many small grocers *(épiceries)* never seem to close. Note, however, that some smaller shops close on Monday or over lunchtime. During the holiday season between mid-July and late August, many small shops close completely for a few weeks.

WHERE TO SHOP IN PARIS

MARCO POLO HIGHLIGHTS

★ **BARTHÉLEMY**
A paradise for cheese lovers in a tiny space ➤ p. 94

★ **DEBAUVE & GALLAIS**
Chocolaterie that resembles an upscale jewellery store ➤ p. 94

★ **LA SAMARITAINE**
Traditional department store reopened in 2021 after 16 years of closure ➤ p. 96

★ **RUE DU FAUBOURG SAINT-HONORÉ**
The haute couture area of the city ➤ p. 97

★ **PLACE DES VICTOIRES**
Young fashion designers and lots of boutiques ➤ p. 97

★ **SAINT-OUEN**
Marché aux Puces: what must be the world's biggest flea market ➤ p. 101

CHAMPS-ÉLYSÉES
Tourist magnet with major brand flagship stores

Boulevard Pereire

Parc Monceau

Rue du Faubou Saint-Honoré ★

Franklin D. Roosevelt

Arrondissement de Passy

TRIANGLE D'O
The finest haute couture

Jardin du Tocadéro

Bois de Boulogne

A 13

Voie Georges Pompidou

Rue de la Convention

Avenue Émile Zola

Arrondissement de Vaugirard

RUE DU COMMERCE
Tasteful little shopping street with a relaxed atmosphere

Saint-Ouen ★

A1

Boulevard Ney

Arrondissement
de la Buttes-Montmartre

BOULEVARD HAUSSMANN

Gigantic department stores with a touch of luxury

Arrondissement de
l'Opéra

Havre - Caumartin

Boulevard Montmartre

FORUM DES HALLES

Temple to consumerism with over 130 shops and a swimming pool

Parc des
Buttes-Chaumont

Boulevard de Magenta

Place des Victoires ★

Châtelet -
Les Halles

MARAIS

Trendy district with chic clothes shops and concept stores

Jardin des
Tuileries

La Samaritaine ★

Rambu...

Debauve & Gallais ★

Arrondissement de
l'Hôtel de Ville

Barthélemy ★

Boulevard Saint-Germain

Saint-Placide

Jardin du
Luxembourg

Jardin des
Plantes

UE DE RENNES

ll the usual suspects

RUE D'ALÉSIA

Outlet paradise

Boulevard Auguste
Blanqui

Arrondissement
des Gobelins

Alésia

1 km
0.62 mi

Opening hours are only listed in this section if they differ from the general rules mentioned on page 88.

ANTIQUES

1 COLLECTED ET AUTRES PHOTGRAPHIES

The digital age seems to have passed this shop by. Photographer Fabien Breuvart sells photos from the previous century; they cost between a few and several hundred euros and are sorted by size and carefully wrapped in transparent foil. The wall next to the front door of the shop serves as an exhibition space for a range of different photo projects. *Fri–Sun | 35–37 rue Charlot | M 8 Filles du Calvaire | 3rd arr. | ⌐ N7*

2 VILLAGE SAINT-PAUL

Around 90 different shops are located in several idyllic interconnected courtyards near the Place des Vosges. You'll find small pieces of furniture, paintings, jewellery, porcelain and more. *Wed–Mon | between rue Saint-Paul & rue Charlemagne | Facebook: Village Saint Paul | M 1 Saint-Paul | 4th arr. | ⌐ N8*

3 DROUOT

As one of the oldest auction houses in the world, Drouot is an institution. Furniture and art objects come under the hammer in 16 halls. Like a visit to a museum! *9 rue Drouot | drouot.com | M 8, 9 Richelieu-Drouot | 9th arr. | ⌐ L5*

BOOKS & MUSIC

4 LES BOUQUINISTES ⚑

The green wooden boxes on both sides of the Seine have shaped the cityscape for more than 300 years. It's a real kick to rummage through the old books, newspapers and postcards. *Between Jardin des Tuileries & Île Saint-Louis | M 7 Pont Neuf | 1st arr./ 5th arr. | ⌐ K–M 7–8*

5 FNAC ☂

The largest bookseller in Paris also has a large CD and DVD department. The Champs-Élysées branch is an excellent place to while away a few hours on a rainy day, or try one of the other 10 Paris outlets. *Mon–Sat until 10.30pm, Sun until 8.45pm | 74 av. des Champs-Elysées | fnac.com | M 1, 9 Franklin D. Roosevelt | 8th arr. | ⌐ G6*

WHERE TO START?

If you're not looking for cheap clothing or practically unwearable haute couture and want to avoid the stress of department store clutter, you're best off in **Marais** *(⌐ M–O 6–8)*. You'll find plenty of shops where Parisians buy their working day wardrobe. Select hand-crafted items and cosmetics, and round off your shopping spree with a break at one of the street cafés in the district. This always turns shopping into a pleasurable event.

Enjoy the smell before you taste the produce at Izraël

DELICATESSENS

6 LEGRAND FILLES & FILS
A mouth-watering delicatessen situated between the nostalgic Galleries Vivienne and rue de la Banque. The shop was established in 1880 and exudes time-honoured elegance. Wine connoisseurs in particular will clamour to experience the extensive wine selection, with tastings at the bar's wooden counters. *1 rue de la Banque | caves-legrand.com | M 1, 7 Palais-Royal-Musée du Louvre | 2nd arr. | ᗌ L6*

7 MAISON STOHRER 🏴
What a dream! This shop is like a blast from the past. The oldest confectionary in Paris was established in 1730 by the court pastry chef of Louis XV. Even today, delicacies such as the *baba au rhum* are made according to the old recipes. Absolutely unbeatable are the savoury options – choose the salmon and spinach for something special. *Mon–Sat 8am–8.30pm, Sun 8am–8pm | 51 rue Montorgueil | stohrer.fr | M 3 Sentier | 2nd arr. | ᗌ L7*

> **INSIDER TIP**
> **What quiche should taste like!**

8 IZRAËL
Specialities from all over the world, mainly Arab, African and Asian countries, are piled to the rafters in wild confusion amid the sausages hanging from hooks and the exotic spices. A unique aromatic experience. *30 rue François Miron | M 1 Saint-Paul | 4th arr. | ᗌ N8*

9 MARIAGE FRÈRES
The original source for top-quality tea blends from this internationally renowned, traditional Parisian brand,

which is sold all over the world. You can sample a steaming brew in the adjoining tea salon, decorated in elegant colonial style. The little tea museum on the first floor bears witness to the company's long history. *30 rue du Bourg-Tibourg | mariagefreres.com | M 1, 11 Hôtel de Ville | 4th arr. | ⊞ F5*

🔟 MAISON DE THÉ GEORGE CANNON

You can choose from over 250 types of tea here. The venerable establishment is much more than a tea shop. In addition to tastings in the bar, light organic dishes are served in the salon. Shiatsu massages or an authentic Japanese tea ceremony on the shop's lower level are a good way to unwind. *12 Notre-Dame-des Champs | georgecannon.fr | M 4 St.-Placide | 6th arr. | ⊞ J10*

🔟 BARTHÉLEMY ⭐

Former President Charles de Gaulle once remarked: "How can anyone govern a nation that has more kinds of cheese than days of the year?" This shop, one of the best cheese emporiums (crèmeries) in Paris, also caters to the Élysée Palace. The aromas of the cheeses waft through the small store. *51 rue de Grenelle | M 12 rue du Bac | 7th arr. | ⊞ J8*

🔟 DEBAUVE & GALLAIS ⭐

The opulent, 200-year-old *chocolaterie* can be compared to a jewellery shop. The big difference: these gems melt in your mouth. *30 rue des Saint-Pères | debauve-et-gallais.com | M 4 Saint-Germain-des-Prés | 7th arr. | ⊞ K8*

🔟 FAUCHON

Seventh heaven for foodies that leaves nothing to be desired. Even the average customer will enjoy treating themselves, sampling a few appetisers on the spot or stocking up to take home. The jelly fruits are something else, as are the truffles and caviar and, of course, the *macarons*. *26 pl. de la Madeleine | fauchon.fr | M 8, 12, 14 Madeleine | 8th arr. | ⊞ J6*

🔟 LADURÉE

The king of *macarons*. Apart from traditional flavours like chocolate, vanilla, coffee, orange blossom or rose, you'll also find seasonal varieties here, like violet or cinnamon. Also worth a visit: the magnificent 19th-century *salon de thé*, with its opulent ceiling frescoes. *Mon–Fri 8.30am–8pm, Sat 9am–8pm, Sun 9.30am–7pm | 16–18 rue Royale | laduree.fr | M 8, 12, 14 Madeleine | 8th arr. | ⊞ J6*

🔟 ROSE BAKERY

The absolute "in" place among young and dynamic Parisian *bobos* (short for bourgeois bohemians), who love the English-style baked goods or the imaginative vegetarian snacks, made with organic ingredients in minimalist surroundings. *Daily 10am–4pm, takeaway until 7pm | 46 rue des Martyrs | rosebakery.fr | M 12 Saint-George | 9th arr. | ⊞ L4*

🔟 DU PAIN ET DES IDÉES

"Bread and ideas" is run by baker Christophe Vasseur. Instead of baguettes and a whole host of different types of bread, he sells a small

The finest caviar is just one of the delicacies on offer at gourmet paradise Fauchon

selection of homemade breads. The classic option is *Le pain des amis* ("bread of friends"). Tourists from all over the world flock to the bakery, built in 1870, not to sample the best croissant in town, but the best in the world. *Mon–Fri | 34 rue Yves Toudic | dupainetdesidees.com | M 5 Jacques Bonsergent | 10th arr. | ⌁ N6*

17 LAVINIA

The ultimate wine shop, with 6,500 wines from more than 30 countries on three floors, at prices ranging from under 10 euros to several thousand. Large selection of organic wines. You can test the wine (without a surcharge) together with a snack of cold meat or cheese in the accompanying bar. *22 av. Victor Hugo | lavinia.com | M 1, 2, 6, RER A Charles de Gaulle-Etoile | 16th arr. | ⌁ E5*

18 DEHILLERIN

In this two-floor shop, open since 1820 and steeped in tradition, you will find everything that has to do with kitchens and cooking. Dehillerin is world-renowned among chefs, and French celebrity chefs are among the customers. *18 & 20 rue Coquillière | e-dehillerin.fr | M 1, 4, 7, 11, 14 Châtelet, RER A, B, D Châtelet-Les Halles | 1st arr. | ⌁ L7*

19 ARTY DANDY

A shop for those who have everything. It sees itself as a gallery-store, and anything in terms of art, kitsch, fashion, cosmetics and design, including individual artworks and limited editions, can be bought here. *1 rue de Furstemberg | artydandy.com | M 4 Saint-Germain-des-Prés | 6th arr. | ⌁ K8*

20 TESTEUR DE COMMERCE

INSIDER TIP
New ideas

This shop sells what producers hope will be the next big thing. People with a business idea can test the sales of their products for a few weeks or months before they take the plunge and open their own shop. *14 rue du Château d'Eau | Facebook: Testeurdecommerce | M 5 Jacques Bonsergent | 10th arr. | ⌐ N6. Other branch: 67 rue Sedaine | 11th arr. | ⌐ P8*

21 BOHÊME

They are not extinct yet, the bohemians! Three or four times a year, hordes of them come together at this artisan market in a former cardboard factory in the fashionable north of Paris. For two days, you can join them to buy creations from a whole host of fashion designers, jewellers, illustrators and designers.

INSIDER TIP
Meet the makers

Perfect if you prefer to avoid mass-produced goods in favour of small treasures with an individual touch! Dates announced on the website. *71 rue de la Fontaine au Roi | hotel-boheme.fr | M 2 Couronnes | 11th arr. | ⌐ P6*

22 MARCHÉ SAINT PIERRE

Covering five floors and over 2,599m sq, this somewhat older department store stocks rolls of fabric at unbeatable prices. Many women from the nearby African neighbourhood scour the shelves for the right materials. Rows of fabric shops line the whole area in this paradise for those who sew. *2 rue Charles Nodier | marchesaintpierre.com | M2 Anvers | 18th arr. | ⌐ L3*

DEPARTMENT STORES

23 LA SAMARITAINE ★

Paris had to wait a long 16 years before this traditional department store, originally founded in 1870, finally reopened its doors in 2021. Alongside shopping, this top address right on the banks of the Seine now also houses a luxury hotel, social housing, offices and a nursery. *19 rue de la Monnaie | lasamaritaine.com | M 7 Pont Neuf | 1st arr. | ⌐ L7–8*

24 LE BON MARCHÉ

The oldest department store in Paris and a symbol of luxury and quality for over 150 years. It is still a joy to meander through this Belle-Époque gem with unobtrusive classical music in the back-ground, away from the usual touristy hustle and bustle. One of the best shoe and fashion departments in town. The *gourmet food section (lagrandeepicerie.fr)* next to it is quite an experience! *24 rue de Sèvres | lebonmarche.com | M 10, 12 Sèvres Babylone | 7th arr. | ⌐ J9*

25 GALERIES LAFAYETTE

The shrine to consumerism, with its massive glass dome, has been a huge attraction since 1908. Clothing is arranged by brand name, as opposed to the type of garment (trousers, shirts, and so on). The shoe department is said to be the largest in the world, covering nearly 3,000sq m. If you need a break from shopping, there's a variety of restaurants and a 🐖 free roof terrace with a panoramic view. *galerieslafayette.com* | *40 bd. Haussmann* | *M 3, 7, 8 Opéra, RER A Auber* | *9th arr.* | *□ K5. Branches: 60 av. des Champs-Élysées* | *8th arr.* | *□ G6. Beaugrenelle shopping centre* | *7 rue Linois* | *15th arr.* | *□ D9*

26 LE PRINTEMPS

In addition to the huge cosmetics department on the ground floor and the beautiful spa area downstairs, the upper floor is devoted to all the luxury fashion brands as well as less costly labels beyond the café-restaurant under the famous Art Nouveau glass dome. *printemps.com* | *64 bd. Haussmann* | *M 3, 9 Havre-Caumartin, RER A Auber* | *9th arr.* | *□ K5. Branches: Carrousel du Louvre* | *99, rue de Rivoli* | *1st arr.* | *□ K7. 21–25 cours de Vincennes* | *12th arr.* | *□ S9*

FASHION & ACCESSORIES

On ⭐ 🚩 *rue du Faubourg Saint-Honoré* (*□ H–K 5–6*) and in the "Triangle d'Or" between the *avenue des Champs-Élysées*, the *avenue Montaigne* (*□ G6*) and *avenue George V* (*□ F6*) you'll find all the well-known names in fashion: Armani, Chanel, Dior, Gucci, Hermès, Lacroix, Max Mara, Versace, and so on. Younger and bolder fashion labels are located around the ⭐ *Place des Victoires* (*□ L6*) and in the boutiques on *rue Etienne Marcel*. Also in the Marais, especially in and around *rue des Francs-Bourgeois* (*□ N–O8*) and the

Christian Lacroix on rue du Faubourg Saint Honoré

surrounding area, are more unconventional fashion boutiques, such as *Abu d'abi* (*aboudabibazar.com*), *Azzedine Alaia* (*alaia.fr*) and sustainable fashion outlets, for example, *Zen Ethic* (*zenethic.com*).

The term *prêt-à-porter* literally means "ready to wear" and refers to industrially produced garments. *Haute couture*, meanwhile, refers to expensive, hand-crafted, made-to-measure garments. Fewer than 20 fashion houses are allowed to adorn their shops with this label. This exclusive circle is selected according to a strict set of criteria set by the Ministry of Economics.

Bargain hunters will be interested in the *degriffé* offers: reduced-price

The shops of perfumery chain Séphora are always vibrant and appealing

brand-name clothing from the previous season from which most of the company labels have been removed.

INSIDER TIP
High quality, lower price

A group of these cheaper shops, some of which also offer outlet items, is located on the *rue d'Alésia* (🕮 *J12*), including *Sonja Rykiel* (no. 110–112) and *Zapa* (no. 139). Some labels are marked down by 40 per cent or even more during clearance sales.

27 CHRISTIAN LOUBOUTIN

The dizzying high heels designed by Christian Louboutin, with equally dizzying price tags and trademark red soles, look their best in the window of the designer's first Parisian boutique. *19 rue Jean-Jaques Rousseau, Galerie Véro Dodat | christianlouboutin.com | M 1 Louvre-Rivoli | 1st arr. | 🕮 L7*

28 GERARD DAREL

One of the major affordable French fashion labels for women's clothing. The trousers, dresses and jackets exude a sporty elegance. *41 rue des Francs-Bourgeois | gerarddarel.com | M 1 Saint Paul | 4th arr. | 🕮 N8*

29 MONIC

This small jewellery store in one of the most lively shopping streets in the Saint-Germain-des-Prés district prides itself on its assortment of more than 10,000 pieces of jewellery, with prices between 1 and 10,000 euros. *14 rue de l'ancienne Comédie | bijouxmonic. com | M 4, 10 Odéon | 6th arr. | 🕮 N8*

30 CHERCHEMINIPPES

Second-hand clothes across five shops: pick your way through well-preserved brand-name pieces, vintage gear and even haute couture items. *Mon–Sat 11am–7pm | 102–114 rue du Cherche-Midi | chercheminippes.com | M 10 Vaneau | 6th arr. | ⬚ J10*

31 L'ECLAIREUR

This shop has an interesting concept, with a mix of designer homewares, jewellery, and clothes by names such as Issey Miyake, Prada, Helmut Lange and Comme des Garçons. *10 rue Boissy d'Anglas | leclaireur.com | M 1, 8, 12 Concorde | 8th arr. | ⬚ J6*

32 AFRICA FIRST

Sika and Jean-Charles first trialled their concept at the Testeur de Commerce (see p. 96) before making the leap during the pandemic. Whether you are looking for fashion, accessories, cosmetics or decor, this is the spot for the latest craze from Africa. *Tue–Sat | 103 rue du Faubourg Saint-Denis | Facebook: Africa First | M 4, 5, 7, Gare de l'Est | 10th arr. | ⬚ M5*

33 EMMAÜS 🐷

A social institution founded by Abbé Pierre selling second-hand clothes, books, crockery, furniture and a whole host of bargains. *Mon–Sat 11am–7.30pm | 54 rue de Charonne | emmaus-alternatives.org | M 8 Ledru-Rollin | 11th arr. | ⬚ P9*

34 DÉPÔT VENTE DE PASSY

The Dépôt sells luxury brands at outlet prices and good bargains are guaranteed. *14 rue de la Tour | depot-vente-luxe.fr | M 6, 9 Trocadéro | 16th arr. | ⬚ D8*

35 SÉPHORA

Giant cosmetic and perfume emporium from the chain of the same name where makeup is applied nonstop as hot disco rhythms play in the background – for free. The chain store's own brand of bath and body products are colourful and pretty. *Daily 10am–9.30pm | 70–72 av. des Champs-Elysées | sephora.fr | M 1, 2, 6, RER A Charles de Gaulle-Etoile | 8th arr. | ⬚ G6*

36 FRAGONARD

Sniff away! The 🐷 *Musée du Parfum (free admission)* of the traditional perfume label Fragonard, from Grasse in the South of France, is situated in an opulent *palais* near the Opéra Garnier. The aim of this operation is, of course, to get you to buy perfume in the showroom at the end of your visit. *Mon–Sat 9am–5.30pm, Sun 9–4.30pm | 9 rue Scribe | musee-parfum-paris.fragonard.com | M 3, 7, 8 Opéra | 9th arr. | K5*

37 ABC DU PARFUM

Create your own perfume! Specially designed workshops will introduce you to the secrets of scents. And after your hour-and-a-half course in all things scenting and smelling, you can take your very own fragrance home with you. *7 rue Vineuse | abcduparfum.fr | M 6 Passy | 16th arr. | ⬚ E8*

ART GALLERIES

Look out for spontaneous, one-off art events. Websites like *lookfindlove.com* post temporary art and design sales at spontaneously chosen locations. *Art éphémère* – street art or graffiti – is always popular, and stencil art *(pochoirs)* on the streets of Paris is also cool. For plans and current spots, see *trompe-l-oeil.info* and *urbanart-paris.fr*.

The largest assortment of galleries for contemporary art is in the vicinity of the art academy on the *rue de Seine* and its side streets, namely, *rue des Beaux Arts*, *rue Jacques Callot* and *rue Mazarine* (*□ K–L8*).

A similar cluster of galleries is found on *rue Vieille du Temple* (*□ N7–8*) and *rue Quincampoix* (*□ M7*).

38 ART GÉNÉRATION

Paris is known as the city of art. Why not acquire an original as a souvenir? In the vicinity of the Centre Pompidou you can choose from paintings, photographs and graphic art from 25 euros upwards! *Tue–Sat 11am–7pm, Sun 2–7.30pm | 67 rue de la Verrerie | artgeneration.fr | M 1, 11 Hôtel de Ville | 4th arr. | □ M8*

39 VIADUC DES ARTS

Artists and craftsmen have set up studios beneath the viaduct's 60 brick arches. Equally inspiring cafés and restaurants offer refreshment among the approx. 130 shops. *1–129 av. Daumesnil | leviaducdesarts.com | M 1, 5, 8 Bastille | 12th arr. | □ O–P 9–10*

MARKETS

Nearly every district in Paris has its own weekly market, including some *marchés biologiques* – organic

markets. For example, *Marché biologique des Batignolles (Sat 9am–3pm | bd. des Batignolles | M 2 Rome, M 2, 13 Place de Clichy | 8th arr./17th arr. | □ J3–4)* or *Marché biologique Brancusi (Sat 9am–3pm | pl. Constantin Brancusi | M 13 Gaîté | 14th arr. | □ K10).*

40 MARCHÉ DES ENFANTS ROUGES ⚑

Paris's oldest food market is inconspicuous. Small, colourful and lively, it's hidden behind houses at the upper end of Le Marais. You'll find more than just stands selling groceries here; there are also lots of little restaurants and street food stalls. The Moroccan food stand

INSIDER TIP
Just like in Morocco

Couscous is highly recommended. *Tue/Wed, Fri/Sat 8.30am–8.30pm, Thu 8.30am–9.30pm, Sun 8.30am–5pm | M 8 Filles du Calvaire | 3rd arr. | □ N7*

41 MARCHÉ BARBÈS 🚩

Eclectic Arab-African weekly bazaar. Prices are low and it's often chaotic, but vibrant bustle is guaranteed. *Wed & Sat mornings | bd. de la Chapelle | M 2, 4 Barbès-Rochechouart | 18th arr. | 🕮 M3*

FLEA MARKETS

42 ALIGRE

The very beautiful Marché d'Aligre is the oldest flea market in Paris. The prices are quite affordable and even groceries can be purchased here. *Tue–Sun mornings | 1e pl. d'Aligre | M 8 Ledru-Rollin | 12th arr. | 🕮 P9*

43 VANVES

The Marché aux Puces de la Porte de Vanves, covering no more than two streets, is the smallest flea market in Paris. On one street, you'll find a mix of new and old clothes, shoes and handbags, while the other one is a haven for novelties and furniture of all kinds. *Sat/Sun 7am–2pm | av. Georges Lafenestre & av. Marc Sangnier | puces devanves.fr | M 13 Porte de Vanves | 14th arr. | 🕮 O*

44 SAINT-OUEN ⭐

With more than 3,000 stalls, the *Marché aux Puces de Saint-Ouen* is the world's largest flea market. You can purchase almost everything here. The grounds at the Porte de Clignancourt encompass a range of 15 markets. To see them all you'll have to cover around 10 miles. For a bit of refreshment along the way, we recommend the rustic tavern *Chez Louisette (130, av. Michelet)* with live music, on the Marché Vernaison. *Mon 11am–5pm, Fri 8am–noon, Sat/Sun 10am–6pm | marcheauxpuces-saintouen.com | M 4 Porte de Clignancourt | 18th arr. | 🕮 K–L1*

All sorts of bright and colourful objects are on sale at Marché aux Puces de Saint-Ouen

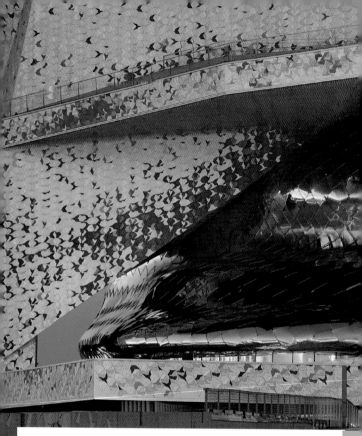

NIGHTLIFE

Trends come and go very quickly in Paris. As soon as a district has been discovered by tourists, Paris nightlife moves elsewhere. The tendency is to migrate further east, where a bar scene has put down roots in the area around the still-affordable artists' flats. Another district that has been branché (hip) for some time is the almost small-town-like Butte-aux-Cailles, with its many bars and relatively reasonable prices.

Pleasure-seekers should be aware that public transport does not operate all night (see p. 148). After 2am, you'll get to your bed by

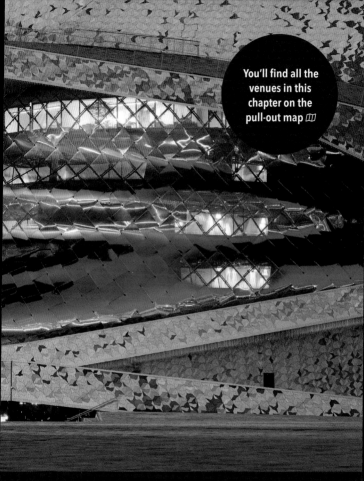

You'll find all the venues in this chapter on the pull-out map 📖

Philharmonie de Paris

night bus, taxi or VTC (see p. 150), or a Vélib (see p. 149). Obviously, there are loads of posh nightclubs and discos in Paris, guarded by strict doormen. However, these days, the latest hotspots are popping up in the city's more industrial locations. Temporary bars move into abandoned factory buildings for a short time before the factories are torn down and replaced with sleek new buildings. Paris nightlife can be expensive: cover charges – depending on the day of the week and event – can easily cost 20 euros. Note that many venues are closed for the month of August.

WHERE TO GO OUT IN PARIS

PIGAL

Sex shops, bars and, course, Le Mou Rou

Le Carmen ★ Ⓜ Pigalle

Boulevard de Courcelles

Parc Monceau

Av. des Champs-Élysées

Arrondissement de l'Élysée

New Morning ★

Rex Club ★ 📍

SAINT-GERMAIN-DES-PRÉS

Classic nightlife spot for the stylish

Jardin des Tuileries

Arrondissement du Louvre

Boulevard de Séba...

Le Perchoir ★

Boulevard Saint-Germain

Cluny-La-Sorbonne Ⓜ

Jardin du Luxembourg

Arrondissement du Panthéon

Place M...

Boulevard Auguste Blanqui

Corvisart Ⓜ

Arrondissement de l'Observatoire

Parc Montsouris

MARCO POLO HIGHLIGHTS

★ LE PERCHOIR
The Parisians conquer the rooftops of their city ➤ p. 106

★ REX CLUB
Huge disco and the best techno club in Paris ➤ p. 108

★ LE CARMEN
Exclusive club in Belle-Époque style ➤ p. 109

★ LA DAME DE CANTON
A musical evening on a Seine boat ➤ p. 110

★ NEW MORNING
Where the world's best jazz musicians play ➤ p. 111

★ PHILHARMONIE DE PARIS
Acoustic delight in a contemporary setting ➤ p. 113

La Villette

Philharmonie de Paris ★

CANAL SAINT-MARTIN
Picnic until late in the evening

Avenue Jean Jaurès

Boulévard de la Chapelle

Ⓜ Jaurès

Parc des Buttes-Chaumont

Boulevard de

BELLEVILLE
Bustling artists' quarter with a multicultural vibe

Ⓜ Pyrénées

Arrondissement de Ménilmontant

Ménilmontant

Ⓜ Oberkampf

RUE OBERKAMPF
The place for party animals

Boulevards des Maréchaux

PLACE DE LA BASTILLE
An impressive number of bars and clubs!

Ⓜ Bastille

Rue du Faubourg Saint-Antoine

Ⓡ Quai d'Austerlitz

Arrondissement de Reuilly

QUARTIER LATIN
Young and buzzing student quarter

Parc de Bercy

La Dame de Canton ★

Parc Zoologique de Paris

BUTTE AUX CAILLES
A small-town feel, with many bars and rustic-style restaurants

1 km
0.62 mi

BARS

Beer, please, but make it cheap! The app and website *Mister Good Beer (mistergoodbeer.com)* has an interactive map of bars with beer prices ranging from just under 3 to 8 euros – including information on whether that's the regular price or just for happy hour.

◪ CHEZ JEANNETTE

When Jeanette was still running the show, workers and prostitutes used to stop here for a bite. Today, this bistro is a trendy hot spot. *Daily | 47 rue du Faubourg-Saint-Denis | tel. 01 47 70 30 89 | FB: @chez.jeannette | M 4, 8, 9 Strasbourg-Saint-Denis | 10th arr. | ⌑ M5*

◪ JESUSPARADIS

Jesus + Paradise = the best caipirinha in Paris. But Jesus here is a woman

---

WHERE TO START?

Nightlife in the Bastille quarter can get wild, particularly on **rue de Lappe** and **rue de la Roquette** (⌑ O8-9). Farther north, along the **Canal Saint-Martin** (⌑ N-O 5-6) and the **Canal de l'Ourcq** (⌑ P2-3), people spread out picnic blankets as soon as the weather permits. Multicultural **Belleville** (⌑ P-Q 5-6) is in the same area. The nightlife on the left bank of the Seine, in the **Saint-Germain-des-Prés** (⌑ J-K 8-9) quarter, is somewhat more subdued.

---

with an afro from Cape Verde. When the sun is shining, young, hip Paris flocks to the terrace in this small pedestrianised arcade. Brazilian tapas and happy hour from 5pm to 8pm makes for an excellent start to the evening. *Mon-Sat 5pm-1.30am | 4 passage du Marché | tel. 09 81 29 72 59 | jesusparadis.fr | M 4, 8, 9 Strasbourg-Saint-Denis | 10th arr. | ⌑ M-N5*

◪ LE PERCHOIR ★

For a long time, the rooftops of Paris were the exclusive preserve of the wealthy and beautiful. Then Adrien Boissaye, who took his regular smoke breaks on a rooftop terrace with a view of the Sacré-Coeur, came up with the idea to open a rooftop bar here. Parisians were soon beating down his door *(restaurant Mon-Fri, bar Mon-Sat 6pm-2am, Sun 4pm-midnight | 14 rue Crespin du Gast | M 2 Ménilmontant | 11th arr. | ⌑ P7)*. Which is why he also opened Perchoir on the rooftops of the *BHV Marais* department store *(Mon-Sat 8.15pm-2am, Sun 7.15pm-2am | 37 rue de la Verrerie | M 1, 11 Hôtel de Ville | 4th arr. | ⌑ M8)* and the *Gare de l'Est (summer Tue-Fri 6pm-1.30am, Sat 4pm-1.30am | 10 place du 11 Novembre 1918 | M 4, 5, 7 Gare de l'Est | 10th arr. | ⌑ N5). leperchoir.fr*

◪ CAFÉ CHARBON

The former coal merchant premises from the early 19th century is an institution, and always full. From the small terrace, you'll have a perfect view of rue Oberkampf, which is famous for its

It's all in the name: Café Charbon was once a coal shop

nightlife. *Daily 8am-2am | 109 rue Oberkampf | tel. 01 43 57 55 13 | lecafecharbon.fr | M 3 Parmentier | 11th arr. | ⫘ P6*

5 ZÉRO ZÉRO

Tiny little bar where different DJs spin every night of the week. The walls are covered in graffiti and the atmosphere is boozy and fun. Speciality of the house: a mix of vodka and ginger named after the bar. For just a few euros, it will help you forget your claustrophobia caused by the bar's close quarters... *Mon-Fri 6pm-2am, Sat 8pm-2am | 89 rue Amelot | FB: Zéro Zéro | M 8 Saint-Sébastien-Froissart | 11th arr. | ⫘ O7*

INSIDER TIP
Try the house cocktail

6 GROUND CONTROL

Paris starts feeling a bit like Berlin here. Partygoers have been making their way for a few years now to this spot in and around the old railway warehouse next to the Gare de Lyon for food (large food court), drinks (several bars) and partying (DJs and concerts). But you're also welcome just to hang out in the sun, browse for books or records or visit Antoine at *Cut Control* for a haircut. *Wed/Thu noon-midnight, Fri/Sat noon-1am, Sun noon-10.30pm | 81 rue du Charolais | groundcontrolparis.com | M 1, 14, RER A Gare de Lyon | 12th arr. | ⫘ P10*

INSIDER TIP
New haircut anyone?

7 LE SOCIAL BAR

Bored of everyone ignoring you in favour of their phones and social media? No need to worry about that here! The bar sees itself as a bit of a social experiment, and founders David, Maeva and Renaud have conjured up various plans to get their guests talking. Some days, you have to let someone else throw a dice to determine the price of your drink. Scored the highest price? Don't sweat it! 50 per cent of the profits is donated to social causes. *Closed Mon evenings, Sun | 25 rue Villiot | tel. 06 72 98 69 05 | social-bar.org | M 1, 14, RER A Gare de Lyon | 12th arr. | ⌐ P10*

8 VILLA M

Paris has a new rooftop bar. The prices notwithstanding – cocktails clock in at more than 20 euros a drink – this is paradise: a green oasis crowning a new building complex with a vertical garden façade. It's set in a four-star hotel and perfect for something special. *Tue–Sat 5–10pm | 24–30 bd. Pasteur | tel. 01 70 61 70 40 | hotel villam-paris15.com/restaurant-bar | M 6, 12 Pasteur | 15th arr. | ⌐ H10*

9 ICE KUBE BAR

Naturally, Paris has an ice bar. No matter whether it's summer or winter, the temperature in here is a constant –20°C. You'll be given down jackets and gloves before entering, and then you'll have your work cut out for you: you'll have exactly 25 minutes to drink three vodka cocktails and a shot (price: 25 euros). *Tue–Sat from 7pm | 1–5 passage Ruelle | tel. 0142 05 20 00 | kubehotel-paris.com | M2 La Chapelle | 18th arr. | ⌐ N3*

10 CAFÉ CHÉRI(E)

Local pub in the hip Belleville area with lots of regulars who enjoy their drinks alongside laid-back young Parisians. And the size of the crowds is understandable: from Thursday to Sunday from 9pm, a DJ spins tunes. The party goes on all night – or at least until the pub closes at 2am. During happy hour (5–8pm), a large beer costs just 4.50 euros, and if the weather cooperates, you can sip it out on the terrace. *Closed Sun | 44 bd. de la Villette | tel. 09 53 05 93 36 | FB: cafe.cherie | M 2, 11 Belleville | 19th arr. | ⌐ P5*

> **INSIDER TIP**
> **A beer in the sunshine**

11 ROSA BONHEUR

This hip bar in the Parc des Buttes-Chaumont (with other locations on the Seine and in the Bois de Vincennes) has become a victim of its own success. If you don't want to queue for hours outside the closed park in the evening, the best thing to do is find yourself a spot in the beer garden in the afternoon, where you can fortify yourself for the full night of dancing ahead. *Thu/Fri 6pm–midnight, Sat/Sun noon–midnight | 2 allée de la Cascade | entrance after the park closes (8/10pm): large gate opposite 74 rue Botzaris | tel. 01 71 60 29 01 | rosabonheur.fr | M 7 to Botzaris | 19th arr. | ⌐ Q4*

> **INSIDER TIP**
> **Get in early!**

CLUBS & DISCOS

12 REX CLUB ★

Huge disco under the cinema complex. Best techno club in the city for over 30 years, also house, disco, concerts. *Wed–Sat 11.45pm/midnight–7am | 5 bd. Poissonière | tel. 01 42 36 10 96 | M 8, 9 Bonne Nouvelle | rexclub.com | 2nd arr. | ⌐ M6*

Calm before the storm: it's about to get loud at Rex Club

13 LE CARMEN ★

If you are not a fan of snobs, avoid this club! But, if you do give it a chance, you'll be more than impressed by this former luxury brothel with its huge mirrors, tall columns and ornate ceiling that bear witness to the glamour of times gone by. Admission is free – if you make it past the bouncer. *Tue–Sat 6pm–6am | 34 rue Duperré | tel. 01 48 74 33 10 | le-carmen.fr | M 2 Blanche | 9th arr. | ☐ K4*

14 LE BALAJO

An institution on *rue de Lappe* – a street famous for its nightlife – since 1936. The tea dances held every Monday are a throwback to the club's origins: "Balajo" comes from "Bal à Jo", or "Joe's ball". Tuesdays are for salsa, while clubbing is the order of the day for the rest of the week. *Thur–Tue |*

9 rue de Lappe | tel. 01 47 00 07 87 | M 1, 5, 8 Bastille | balajo.fr | 11th arr. | ☐ O8

15 FAVELA CHIC

Dine on Brazilian cuisine and sip caipirinhas in the early evening, then dance on the benches to Latin American beats at night. *Wed–Sat (Fri/Sat until 5am) | 18 rue du Faubourg du Temple | tel. 01 40 21 38 14 | favelachic.com | M 3, 5, 8, 9, 11 République | 11th arr. | ☐ O6*

16 SUPERSONIC

All-in-one bar, club and concert hall. The brick lofts host rock, pop, electro, and hip-hop parties. 🐦 Free concerts during the week, and dancing 'til the sun comes up on weekends. *Sun–Thu 7pm–2am, Fri/Sat 7pm–6am | 9 rue Biscornet | tel. 01 49 23 41 90 |*

supersonic-club.fr | M 1, 5, 8 Bastille
|12th arr. | ⌘ O9

🔟 LA DAME DE CANTON ★

A real Chinese junk on the Seine! This venue is a constant on the Paris music scene: Groups like Louise Attaque, Noir Désir and Bénabar perform here. You can also enjoy a delicious meal on board before the concert starts. *Tue–Sat 7pm–midnight, bar Fri/Sat 7pm–2am, terrace in summer open daily noon–2am | Port de la Gare | tel. 01 53 61 08 49 | damedecanton. com | M 6 Quai de la Gare | M 14, RER C Bibliothèque F. Mitterrand | 13th arr. | ⌘ P12*

🔟 WANDERLUST

Club and concert hall in the futuristic neon-green Cité de la Mode directly on the Seine. It's worth a visit, especially in summer when the terrace and food court are open! *Tue/Wed, Fri 1pm–6am, Thu 6pm–6am, Sun 4pm–1am | 32 quai d'Austerlitz | tel. 06 12 74 07 28 | wanderlustparis. com | M 5, 10, RER C Gare d'Austerlitz | 13th arr. | ⌘ O11*

INSIDER TIP
Party by the Seine

🔟 LE DIVAN DU MONDE & MADAME ARTHUR

Le Divan du Monde, an old Paris theatre with a stage and gallery in the vibrant Pigalle district, has teamed up with its neighbour *Madame Arthur*, a legendary transvestite theatre. The duo has devoted itself entirely to the art of French *chanson*. For 80 euros, you get two cabaret performances

plus dinner and club until the early morning. If that's a bit over budget, standing room without food is available for 20 euros. *Thu–Sat 8pm–6am | 75 rue des Martyrs | tel. 07 68 78 68 01 | madamearthur.fr | M 2, 12 Pigalle | 18th arr. | ⌘ L4*

🔟 LE HASARD LUDIQUE

Another abandoned train station on the former circle line that the Parisians have reclaimed – in the truest sense of the word. Local residents helped develop the concept for cultural centre "The Game of Chance". Regular concerts and parties are held in the ballroom, and *Cantine créative* offers a decent selection of tapas and drinks. Try a local beer with a double meaning, like "À l'Ouest", which means "out west" but also "wasted". *Tue–Thu noon–midnight, Fri/Sat noon–2am, Sun 11.30am–10pm | 128 av. de Saint-Ouen | tel. 01 42 28 35 91 | lehasardludique.paris | M 13 Porte de Saint-Ouen | 18th arr. | ⌘ J1*

INSIDER TIP
Beer made in Paris

JAZZ & LIVE MUSIC

🔟 LE BAISER SALÉ

Jazz cellar with a bar and jazz videos. Relaxed atmosphere with salsa, blues, fusion and funk music. *Daily | 58 rue des Lombards | tel. 01 42 33 37 71 | lebaisersale.com | M 1, 4, 7, 11, 14 Châtelet, RER A, B, D Châtelet-Les Halles | 1st arr. | ⌘ M8*

🔟 AU DUC DES LOMBARDS

Easy-going club highlighting a wide

spectrum of music, from free jazz to hard bop. The bar serves small meals. *Mon–Sat | 42 rue des Lombards | tel. 01 42 33 22 88 | ducdeslombards. com | M 1, 4, 7, 11, 14 Châtelet, RER A, B, D Châtelet-Les Halles | 1st arr. | 🚇 M7*

23 CAVEAU DE LA HUCHETTE

The old walls of a medieval vaulted cellar come to life every evening with live jazz. *Sun–Thu 9pm-2.30am, Fri/ Sat 9pm–4am | 5 rue de la Huchette | tel. 01 43 26 65 05 | caveaudelahuchette.fr | M 4 Saint-Michel, Cité | 5th arr. | 🚇 L9*

24 LE CAVERN

It looks small, but it has a surprise that you can't see from the outside: at the end of the long, narrow room on the ground floor, there's a staircase leading down into a rustic vaulted cellar. Free concerts are held here regularly, and at the weekend, you can party into the wee hours of the morning. *Sun–Thu 5pm–2am, Fri/Sat 5pm–4am | 21 rue Dauphine | tel. 01 43 54 53 82 | lecavernclub.com | M 4, 10 Odéon | 5th arr. | 🚇 L8*

25 NEW MORNING ★

The city's best and most famous jazz club, where renowned international musicians take the stage. *Daily until approx. 1am depending on programme | 7–9 rue des Petites-Ecuries | newmorning.com | M 4 Château d'Eau | 10th arr. | 🚇 M5*

The medieval Caveau de Huchette has been on the nightlife scene for more than 70 years

26 LE BATACLAN

Legendary Paris concert hall and stage that is back on its feet after the terrorist attack of 13 November 2015. The renovations took a year; now, major rock and pop acts from France and around the world are performing here regularly once again. *50 bd. Voltaire | tel. 01 43 14 00 30 | le-bataclan.com | M 5, 9 Oberkampf | 11th arr. | O7*

27 MOONSHINER

This bar is located behind a fridge door in the unassuming Pizzeria Da Vito. Yes, Paris hasn't escaped the global trend for speakeasy bars, inspired by the hidden bars of US Prohibition. This cocktail bar will transport you to 1920s New York. *Daily | 5 rue Sedaine | tel. 09 50 73 12 99 | FB: moonshiner cocktailbar | M 5 Bréguet-Sabin | 11th arr. | O8*

28 LA GARE & LE GORE

An ultra-cool place inside an old train station concourse. The grounds are enchantingly beautiful, with a terrace and garden. Trains haven't stopped here since 1934 – now, jazz acts large and small perform in this club. Free admission. Forced to close during the pandemic, it reopened with new underground electro club Le Gore (admission: *Sun/Mon 5 euros, Tue free, Wed/Thur 10 euros, Fri/Sat 15 euros). Daily, terrace & snacks from noon. La Gare 9pm–1am, Le Gore midnight–6am | 1 av. Corentin Cariou | FB: LaGareLeGore | M 7 Corentin Cariou | 19th arr. | P2*

29 LA BELLEVILLOISE

A 2,000sq m hall dating from the 19th century, with a wonderful potpourri of activity: concerts, art exhibitions and assorted events, plus a café and restaurant. On Sundays there's a superb jazz brunch with a buffet and live music. *Reservation essential (11.30am or 2pm | 32 euros). Restaurant Thur–Sat 6.30pm–1am (8–10pm live music, 2 euros extra), Sun 11.30am–4pm, event rooms depending on programme | 19–21 rue Boyer | tel. 01 46 36 07 07 | labellevilloise.com | M 3 Gambetta | 20th arr. | R6*

INSIDER TIP Jazz with your brunch

CINEMAS

Foreign films, as a rule, are shown in their original language with French subtitles – *VOST (version originale avec sous-titres)* – while films dubbed into French are denoted as *v. f. (version française)*. In addition to the three major chains – *Gaumont Pathé (cinemasgaumontpathe.com)*, *UGC (ugc.fr)* and *MK2 (mk2.com)* – the city also offers many small, independent cinemas *(cip-paris.fr)*.

30 CINÉMATHÈQUE FRANÇAISE

The futuristic building by Frank O. Gehry is a mecca for film fans! There's a *museum (Mon, Wed–Fri noon–7pm, Sat/Sun 11am–8pm | admission 10 euros, special exhibitions 12 euros)* with film posters, costumes and props, an archive with more than 40,000 films, and multiple cinemas. Film history comes to life here. See the online calendar for film times. *Closed Tue | 51 rue de Bercy | cinematheque.fr | M 6, 14 Bercy | 12th arr. | ⫚ P11*

CONCERTS

A number of stages showcase all types of music by top performers and amateurs alike. The city is also an important venue for world music. There are many free events and musicians often play in the parks in July and August.

🗓 OLYMPIA

Legendary, world-famous concert hall open since the 19th century, hosting performers ranging from French celebrities to the Rolling Stones. *28 bd. des Capucines | tel. 0147429488 | olympiahall.com | M 3, 7, 8 Opéra, RER A Auber | 9th arr. | ⫚ J6*

🗓 LA CIGALE

International stars have performed at this venue, including Kevin Costner and his band, Modern West, and Kurt Vile & The Violators. *120 bd. Rochechouart | tel. 01 49 25 89 99 | lacigale.fr | M 2, 12 Pigalle | 18th arr. | ⫚ L4*

🗓 PHILHARMONIE DE PARIS ⭐

The philharmonic hall designed by Jean Novel is a sight for sore eyes, with spectacular architecture including an accessible roof. None of the over 2,400 seats is more than 30m from the stage. The repertoire ranges from classical to world music. The *museum (daily | 9 euros)* is worth seeing, with instruments dating from the Middle Ages to today, and there are also plenty of options for the hungry. Try *L'Atelier* café for a quick bite or *Café*

The name, which means "the cicada", is deceptive. La Cigale rocks!

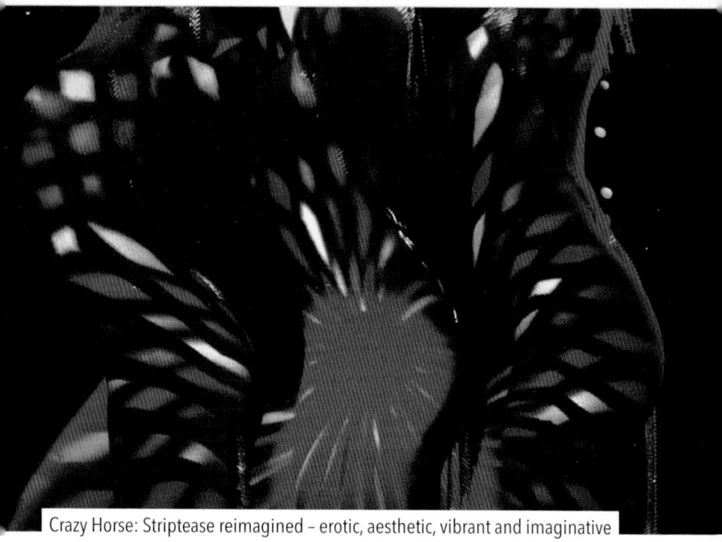

Crazy Horse: Striptease reimagined – erotic, aesthetic, vibrant and imaginative

des concerts (cafedesconcerts.com), where you can also dine. For something fancy, head to the panorama restaurant *Le Balcon (restaurant-le balcon.fr). 221 av. Jean-Jaurès | tel. 01 44 84 44 84 | philharmoniedeparis.fr | M 5 Porte de Pantin | 19th arr. | R2*

34 LE ZÉNITH

This huge concert hall in the Parc de la Villette is a venue for rock and pop concerts accommodating up to 9,000 fans. *211 av. Jean-Jaurès | tel. 01 44 52 54 56 | le-zenith.com | M 5 Porte de Pantin | 19th arr. | R2*

REVUES

35 LE CRAZY HORSE

Sleazy? Not at all! This is eroticism paired with artistic sensibility. A combination of ballet and striptease with beautiful aesthetic effects. *Shows: Sun–Fri 8pm, 10.30pm, Sat 7pm, 9.30pm, 11.45pm | from 90 euros | 12 av. George V | tel. 01 47 23 32 32 | lecrazyhorseparis.com | M 1 George V, M 9 Alma Marceau | 8th arr. | F6*

36 LE MOULIN ROUGE

Lavish revues in the "Red Mill", immortalised by Henri de Toulouse-Lautrec and the birthplace of the cancan, located at the foot of Montmartre. *Shows between 1pm & 11pm | from 88 euros incl. champagne, from 180 euros including lunch, from 205 euros including dinner) | 82 bd. De Clichy | tel. 01 53 09 82 82 | moulin-rouge.fr | M 2 Blanche | 18th arr. | K3*

THEATRE

You'd like to go to the theatre, but don't speak a word of French? *Theatre in Paris (theatreinparis.com) has the answer: English surtitles! All available shows are listed on the website.*

☷ COMÉDIE FRANÇAISE
Founded in 1680 under Louis XIV. Classic theatre in the tradition of Molière. ☛ Seats with an obstructed view are available an hour before the show for just 5 euros; on Mondays everyone under 28 can attend for free. *1 place Colette | tel. 01 44 58 15 15 | comedie-francaise.fr | M 1, 7 Palais Royal–Musée du Louvre | 1st arr. | ⌑ K7*

☷ THÉÂTRE DE LA VILLE
Premier stage in Paris for modern dance, this venue also stages dramatic works and music (especially world music). *2 pl. du Châtelet | tel. 01 42 74 22 77 | theatredelaville-paris.com | M 1, 4, 7, 11, 14 Châtelet, RER A, B, D Châtelet-Les Halles | 4th arr. | ⌑ L8*

☷ THÉÂTRE ÉQUESTRE ZINGARO
Internationally renowned horse choreographer Bartabas offers equestrian sport with an artistic edge. He also runs a riding academy housed in the royal stables of the Palace of Versailles (see p. 68), which can be visited separately *(bartabas.fr/academie-equestre-de-versailles). 176 av. Jean Jaurès, Aubervilliers | bartabas.fr/zingaro | M 7 Fort d'Aubervilliers | ⌑ 0*

CIRCUS

☷ CIRQUE D'HIVER ☻
Over 150 years old, this magnificent circus building is considered one of the most beautiful in the world. The Bouglione family offers the best in circus tradition here. *Shows Sept–March Sat/Sun (every day in the school holidays) | admission 20–64 euros online | 110 rue Amelot | cirquedhiver.com | M 8 Filles du Calvaire | 11th arr. | ⌑ O7*

TOO MUCH LOVE

Proposals, honeymoons, weekends with a sweetheart – lovers from around the world travel to Paris. And how do today's global citizens symbolise their love? With a padlock – or perhaps it's better to call it a lovelock. A heart-shaped one is best, with your initials engraved. They're easy to order online, or you can buy them from street vendors in the city. But you can imagine the situation after decades of lovers attaching their locks to the city's bridges. The pedestrian Pont des Arts bridge had the biggest problem – when part of the handrail collapsed under their weight, the city removed 45 tonnes of these tokens of love and replaced the bridge's latticework with glass panels. But lovers just started hanging their locks on other bridges. Today, signs are posted prohibiting this: "Our bridges won't be able to withstand your love." The metal locks removed from bridges were auctioned off, bringing in 250,000 euros for refugee relief.

ACTIVE & RELAXED

Lunch break in front of the Pavillon de la Reine on Place des Vosges

SPORT & WELLNESS

BOULES

Yes, boules, or *pétanque*, really is a sport! And it's a quintessentially French one at that. Pensioners and wealthy espadrilles-wearing retirees in the south of France aren't the only ones who play – in fact, in Paris, meeting for a game of boules in the summer is the hip new trend.

INSIDER TIP
Aperitif with your boules

Boulodrome, for example, organises tournaments and even hosts boules parties with open-air bars and DJs. *Route des Fortifications | M 8 Porte de Charenton | lesaperosdelapetanque.fr | 12th arr. | ▥ R–S12*

FOOTBALL (WATCHING A GAME)

Head to the *Parc des Princes* to see Paris Saint-Germain's home games. You can also get a behind-the-scenes look on a 👥 stadium tour (25 euros). *24, rue du Commandant Guilbaud | billetterie.psg.fr | M 9 Porte de Saint-Cloud | 16th arr. | ▥ A10–11.*

Has your home team finally made it to the key match of the season? No need to cancel your trip to Paris! You can see English Premier League football in sports bars like the *Rush Bar*. Here, you even tuck into classic pub food like burgers and fish and chips. *32 rue Saint Sébastien | rushbar.fr | M 8 Saint-Sébastien–Froissart | 11th arr. | ▥ O7*

INLINE SKATING 🐷

Every Friday evening thousands of inline skaters whizz along a nearly 30km-long stretch of roads that have been closed to traffic. Start is at 10pm between Montparnasse station and the Montparnasse tower. You're also welcome to join by bike or scooter. *Gare Montparnasse | pari-roller.com | M 4, 6, 12, 13 Montparnasse-Bienvenüe | 14th arr. | ▥ H–J 10–11*

Aquaboulevard is a water-filled playground

SWIMMING 🤽‍♀️ 🏊

The *Aquaboulevard* is one of the largest water parks in Europe, featuring pools with waterfalls and a number of fun waterslides under its glass roof. *Mon–Thu 9am–11pm, Fri 9am–midnight, Sat 8am–midnight, Sun 8am–11pm | admission 27 euros, 3–11s 20 euros | 4 rue Louis Armand | aquaboulevard.com | M 8 Balard | 15th arr. | ▥ D12*

WELLNESS

In France, "Zen" always signals "relaxed". Check out the 🏖️ *Bar à Sieste – Zzz-Zen*. You can relax on a Shiatsu massage lounger and listen to ethereal music played through your headphones. The loungers are separated from each other by either walls or curtains. The most sophisticated Japanese devices knead and massage you for 35 minutes. This costs 22 euros, which is not very much by Paris standards. A cup of organic tea is included. For a bit more pampering, head to the vaulted cellar for a fish pedicure (30 euros) or treat yourself to a manicure (from 25 euros). *Mon–Sat noon–8pm | 29 passage Choiseul | tel. 01 71 60 81 55 | barasieste.com | M 7, 14 Pyramides | 2nd arr. | ▥ K6*

Every morning, dozens of Parisians head to the lovely *Parc des Buttes-Chaumont* (see p. 64) on the eastern side of the city to recharge their batteries with qigong experts. 🏖️ Free of charge whatever the weather and sessions run 365 days a year. If you're an early riser, you won't find a better way to start the day. After an hour of the quiet exercise, the hustle and bustle of the city can't touch you – let's go! *Daily 9–10am | av. de la Cascade diagonally opposite Rosa Bonheur restaurant | M 7 Botzaris | 19th arr. | ▥ Q4*

FESTIVALS & EVENTS

FEBRUARY
Chinese New Year: colourful procession around the Place d'Italie (dates vary)

MARCH
Festival du livre de Paris: The Paris book fair takes the form of a festival. *festivaldulivredeparis.fr*

MARCH-APRIL
Banlieues Bleues: first-rate jazz festival in Saint-Denis and other suburbs. *banlieuesbleues.org*

MAY
Nuit européenne des musées: Many Paris museums take part in the annual European Night of Museums, opening for free in the evening. *nuitdesmusees.culture.gouv.fr*

MAY-JUNE
French Open: Around 60,000 tennis balls get used each year, when the best players meet each other in the Stade Roland-Garros. *rolandgarros.com*

JUNE
★ 🐷 **Fête de la Musique**: free concerts on nearly every street corner in the city, all night long (21/22 June).
Marche des fiertés lesbiennes, gaies, bi et trans: gay, lesbian, bi and trans Pride procession through the centre (fourth Saturday)

JULY
Bastille Day: large military parade on the Champs-Élysées and fireworks on the Place du Trocadéro in the evening, plus formal balls on the 13th or 14th in the city's fire stations (14 July)
Tour de France: final stage on the Champs-Élysées (last or penultimate Sunday)

Bastille Day fireworks in front of the Eiffel Tower

JULY-AUGUST

☛ **Paris Jazz Festival**: free concerts with international jazz greats in the Parc Floral des Bois de Vincennes. *parisjazzfestival.fr*

Paris-Plages: various beach activities for five weeks beginning in mid-July

☛ **Open-air Cinema**: free cinema at Parc de la Villette (from mid-July)

AUGUST

Rock en Seine: rock music greats perform for three days in the Parc de Saint-Cloud. *rockenseine.com*

SEPTEMBER

Journées européennes du patrimoine: free admission to public buildings otherwise closed to the general public (third weekend)

SEPTEMBER-DECEMBER

★ **Festival d'Automne**: autumn festival with theatre, music and dance performances. *festival-automne.com*

OCTOBER

Fête des Vendanges: party to celebrate the grape harvest on Montmartre (first Saturday). *fetedes vendagesemontmatre.com*

Fiac: extensive contemporary art fair. *fiac.com*

Nuit Blanche: music and art happenings all night long, partly in unusual places (usually on the first Saturday)

OCTOBER-NOVEMBER

Paris Games Week: the latest video games are presented in early November. *parisgamesweek.com*

SLEEP WELL

LOVE NEST

Guests at the *Lovehotel (18 rooms | 88 rue Saint-Denis | tel. 07 82 70 27 37 | lovehotelaparis.fr | M 1, 4, 7, 11, 14 Châtelet, RER A, B, D Châtelet-Les Halles | €€€ | 1st arr. | ⛢ M7)* don't come to sleep. Travellers abandon themselves to the magic of Paris

in the *"nids d'amour"* (love nests), bookable by the hour, while Parisians enjoy clandestine love affairs for an hour or two.

AS MANY STYLES AS ROOMS

Hip *Hôtel Edgar (13 rooms | 31 rue d'Alexandrie | tel. 01 40 41 05 19 | edgarparis.com | M 3 Sentier | €€ | 2nd arr. | ⛢ M6)*, with its bar and restaurant, was set up by restaurateur Guillaume Rouget-Luchaire in a former clothes factory in "Silicon Sentier" (see p. 31). The hotel is named for his son, and Rouget-Luchaire has

painstakingly worked out the design of the rooms with creative family members and friends. Discover what happens when documentary filmmakers, visual artists, a stylist from Chanel and a psychotherapist are let loose on a hotel room. Unique, contemporary and very Parisian.

COUNTRY HOUSE & PARK

The *Hôtel des Grandes Écoles (51 rooms | 75 rue du Cardinal Lemoine | tel. 01 43 26 79 23 | hoteldesgrandesecoles.com | M 10 Cardinal Lemoine | €€ | 5th arr. | ⛢ M9)* is an absolute highlight. Who would expect a country house with park-like grounds only a stone's throw from the vibrant rue Mouffetard and Panthéon? Beautifully quiet, each room in the three small buildings is decorated with period furniture. Most rooms have a view of the garden, where you can also enjoy breakfast.

Sleep on a riverboat at OFF Paris Seine

DOWN BY THE RIVER

The first Parisian hotel on the Seine. The *OFF Paris Seine (54 rooms, 4 suites | 20–22 Port d'Austerlitz | tel. 01 44 06 62 65 | offparisseine.com | M 5, 10, RER C Gare d'Austerlitz | €€€ | 13th arr. | ▥ O11)* is stylish and modern, with lots of metal, glass and wood, and is moored in front of the Gare d'Austerlitz. When it comes to the rooms, you have a choice between a view of the hustle and bustle on the riverbank or the Seine. If you want something extra-special, why not reserve the golden-orange Sunset designer suite?

SOLAR HÔTEL

The *Solar (24 rooms | 22 rue Boulard | tel. 01 43 21 08 20 | solarhotel.fr | M 4, 6, RER B Denfert-Rochereau | € | 14th arr. | ▥ J12)* is the first hotel in Paris to call itself "ecological". It not only publicly divulges how much energy it uses, but also endeavours to reduce this figure. Breakfast is 100% organic, and nobody will mind if you bring your own food to eat in the garden. True to form, bicycles are at your disposal for exploring the city.

TOTALLY BONKERS!

At *Chez Bertrand (12 rue Gustave Rouanet | tel. 06 63 19 19 87 | chezbertrand.com, paris-champion.de, paris-circus.de | M 4 Porte de Clignancourt | € | 18th arr. | ▥ L1)*, you might find your toilet in a disused telephone booth. The chandelier is made of tennis balls, and the bed is inside an old Citroën 2 CV. The five motley holiday flats managed by Bertrand de Neuville are all located in the north of the city, not far from Montmartre and the Saint-Ouen flea market.

DISCOVERY TOURS

Do you want to get under the skin of the city? Then these discovery tours provide the perfect guide. They include advice on which sights to visit, tips on where to stop for that perfect holiday snap, a choice of the best places to eat and drink and suggestions for fun activities.

Evening at the Arc de Triomphe

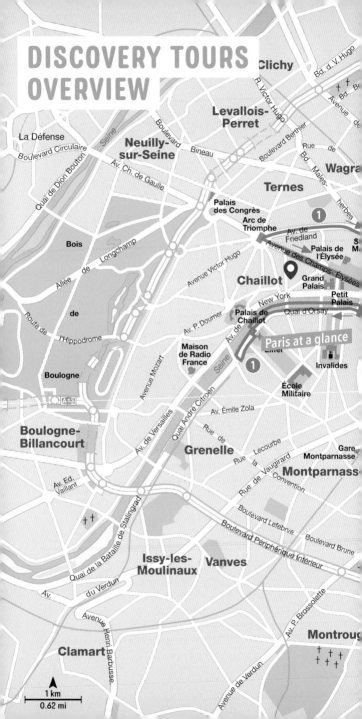

DISCOVERY TOURS OVERVIEW

Clichy

Bd. d. V. Hugo

Levallois-Perret

R. Victor Hugo

Bd.

Avenue de

La Défense

Seine

Boulevard Bineau

Boulevard Berthier

Rue de

Bd. Males-herbes

Wagra

Neuilly-sur-Seine

Boulevard Circulaire

Quai de Dion Bouton

Av. Ch. de Gaulle

Ternes

Palais des Congrès

Arc de Triomphe

Av. de Friedland

S M.

Bois

Allée de Longchamp

Avenue Victor Hugo

Avenue des Champs-Élysées

Palais de l'Élysée

de

Route de l'Hippodrome

Av. P. Doumer

Chaillot

Grand Palais

Petit Palais

New York

Palais de Chaillot

Quai d'Orsay

Boulogne

Avenue Mozart

Maison de Radio France

Seine

Paris at a glance

Av. de

Eiffel

Invalides

École Militaire

Boulogne-Billancourt

Av. Ed. Vaillant

Av. de Versailles

Quai André Citroën

Av. Émile Zola

Grenelle

Rue de

Rue Lecourbe

Rue de la

Rue de Vaugirard

Convention

Gare Montparnasse

Montparnass

Quai de la Bataille de Stalingrad

Boulevard Lefebvre

Boulevard Brune

Boulevard Périphérique Intérieur

Issy-les-Moulinaux

Vanves

Av.

du Verdun

Avenue Henri Barbusse

Av. P. Brossolette

Clamart

Avenue de Verdun

Montroug

▲
1 km
0.62 mi

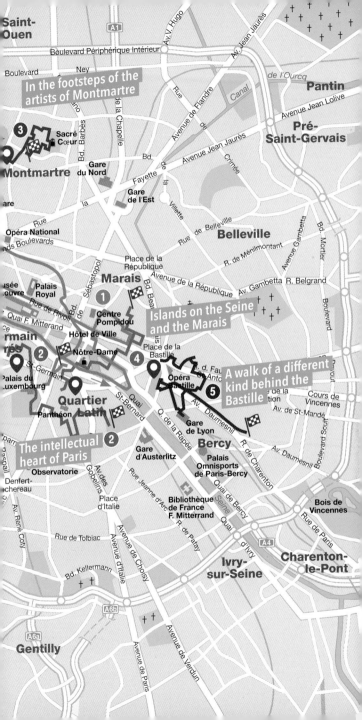

❶ PARIS AT A GLANCE

➤ Stroll along the Champs-Élysées
➤ The Eiffel Tower seen from the Seine
➤ A wonderful view over the city

📍	Fouquet's	🏁	Caveau de la Huchette
→	27.5km	🚶	1 day (3 hours total walking time)

ℹ️ Costs: Métro/bus tickets approx. 8 euros, Bato-bus ticket 17 euros, admission to the Musée d'Orsay 16 euros, Arc de Triomphe 13 euros
Nearest Métro to the start of the tour on the Champs-Élysées: M 1 George V
Reserve a table for dinner at ❾ Bouillon Racine ahead
The nearest Métro station to the last stop on the tour on rue de la Huche: M 4 Saint-Michel or Cité

MAGNIFICENT AVENUE, MAGNIFICENT BUILDINGS

❶ Fouquet's

Start your day with breakfast on the Champs-Élysées ➤ p. 48. One of the most famous of the many cafés is ❶ Fouquet's (daily | no. 99 | 8th arr. | tel. 01 40 69 60 50 | €€€). Film stars celebrate the annual César awards here. The hustle and bustle along this boulevard, with the Arc de Tri-omphe in the background, is a fitting start for a walk through Paris.

❷ Place de la Concorde

Ride down this impressive avenue on a no. 73 bus, passing by the glass-roofed Grand Palais and the Petit Palais ➤ p. 50. As you cross ❷ Place de la Concorde ➤ p. 51 with its stately obelisk and gigantic monumental fountains, you will get a feel for the enormity of this square. Before the bus turns, make sure to take a look at the Jardin des Tuileries ➤ p. 34, the oldest park in the city. It links the square with the Louvre complex. After the bus crosses the Seine, get off at the last stop in front

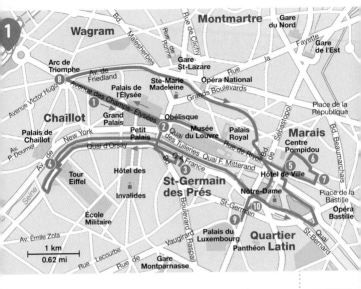

of the ❸ Musée d'Orsay ➤ p. 46. You will surely be delighted by the architecture of this con-verted railway station and the sizeable collection of French Impressionist art that it holds. After a snack at the museum, *take the RER C from the Musée d'Orsay station for three stops to the* Eiffel Tower ➤ p. 44.

❸ Musée d'Orsay

ON THE SEINE TO THE ROYAL PALACE

At the foot of this landmark, *on the* ❹ Pont d'Iéna *bridge, are the boats belonging to the Batobus line dock.* Hop aboard and get to know the city from an entirely new perspective on the Seine. During the trip, the boat glides beneath a number of bridges, including the gilded Pont Alexandre III ➤ p. 50 and the famous Pont Neuf ➤ p. 33 – bringing you to the heart of the city, the islands on the Seine. The long walls of the for-mer royal seat known as the Louvre ➤ p. 33, now the largest museum in the world, stretch along the left-hand side. As the boat circles the islands, you can see if the renovation work has been completed on Notre Dame Cathedral ➤ p. 39.

❹ Pont d'Iéna

Comings and goings on the rue des Rosiers, a typical street in the Marais

⑤ Hôtel de Ville

⑥ Marais

Disembark at the ⑤ Hôtel de Ville ➤ p. 39 stop. Walk from here along *rue de Rivoli and rue Vieille du Temple Vieille du Temple* to the nearby bustling district of ⑥ Marais. Check out the numerous small shops such as a branch of the Uniqlo chain on rue des Francs-Bourgeois (no. 39), with its inexpensive fashion collections. Then take a break in one of the old-style cafés in this quarter. A favourite spot on the impressive former royal square, the Place des Vosges ➤ p. 37, is ⑦ Café Hugo *(daily | no. 22 | 4th arr. | tel. 01 42 72 64 04 | €–€€)*.

⑦ Café Hugo

UNDERGROUND TO THE TRIUMPHAL ARCH

⑧ Arc de Triomphe

Head down to the Métro *at Saint Paul station. Walk down rue de Birague and rue Saint-Antoine to get to the station and then take the M 1 to Charles de Gaulle-Étoile.* This underground route will bring you back to the starting point of the tour, near the ⑧ Arc de Triomphe ➤ p. 48 and its viewing platform. Twelve avenues converge like a star *(étoile)* at Place Charles de Gaulle-Étoile, offering the best overview of the layout of the city. By now, you'll surely be ready for *diner* and you'll hopefully have booked a table at one of the classic Belle-Époque restaurants for which Paris is so well-known.

FROM RESTAURANT TO JAZZ CLUB

A particularly good address is ❾ Bouillon Racine ➤ p. 81 in the old intellectual neighbourhood of Saint-Germain-des-Prés ➤ p. 132. For the fastest way to get there, *take the RER A from Charles de Gaulle-Étoile and change trains Châtelet-Les Halles to the RER B and get off at Saint-Michel.* The floral designs so typical of the Art Nouveau style cover the restaurant, and its menu is equally decorative. Enjoy a leisurely meal here before delving into the lively nightlife in this area. End the day in true Parisian style at one of the most authentic jazz clubs in the district, ❿ Caveau de la Huchette ➤ p. 111.

❾ Bouillon Racine

❿ Caveau de la Huchette

❷ THE INTELLECTUAL HEART OF PARIS

➤ Stroll from gallery to gallery
➤ Spread out your picnic blanket in the Jardin du Luxembourg
➤ Trace the remains of Roman Paris

📍 Les Deux Magots	🚩 Grande Mosquée de Paris
→ 4.8km	🚶 4 hours (1¼ hours total walking time)

ℹ The nearest Métro station to the start of the tour on Place Saint-Germain-des-Prés: M 4 Saint-Germain-des-Prés
The nearest Métro stations to the last stop on the tour on rue Geoffrey Saint-Hilaire: M 7 Place Monge or Censier Daubenton

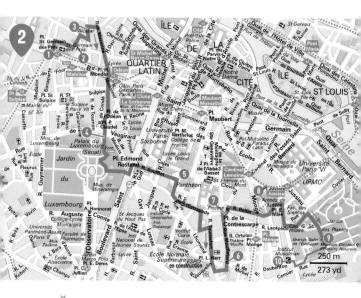

CHURCHES AND CAFÉS, PLACES AND PARKS

① Les Deux Magots

The patio of ① Les Deux Magots ➤ p. 75 is a bit like a box at the theatre, making it the perfect place to start this tour. Sit back and relax as you watch people stroll past, stressed and chilled alike. The 8th-century church of Saint-Germain-des-Prés, one of the oldest in Paris, is just opposite. Rue Bonaparte, like other streets in this area, is full of galleries, antique dealers, fabric shops, cafés and restaurants. *Follow rue de l'Abbaye behind the church* to the romantic, tree-lined square on ② **Rue de Furstemberg**, which was once home to the studio of artist Eugène Delacroix (no. 6) – you can visit for free if you've bought a ticket for the Louvre *(musee-delacroix.fr).*

② Rue de Furstemberg

Then turn right down rue Jacob, which leads to the lively rue de Seine. Stop for coffee on the patio of the ever-popular ③ La Palette *(daily | 43, rue de Seine | tel. 01 43 26 68 15 | lapalette-paris.com | €€). Continue along rue Jacques Callot, then turn right up rue Mazarine, and head over boulevard Saint-Germain to rue de l'Odéon.* Walk past the neoclassical Théâtre de l'Odéon until you come to the ④ Jardin du

③ La Palette

④ Jardin du Luxembourg

Luxembourg ➤ p. 44, one of the most popular parks in Paris. Take in the Palais du Luxembourg, modelled after the Florentine Palazzo Pitti, as you sit on the edge of the pond or the shaded Fontaine de Médicis.

TEMPLE TO THE MIND AND GOURMET SHOPPING

Across from the main entrance, on the other side of the lively Boulevard Saint-Michel, with its street cafés, *follow rue Soufflot* up to the domed ❺ Panthéon ➤ p. 42, a mausoleum in which many French luminaries are buried. The narrow lanes that wind up the Montagne Sainte-Geneviève are part of one of the oldest neighbourhoods in Paris. *Walk along rue Malebranche,* which runs through the trench around a medieval city wall, *rue des Fossés Saint-Jacques* and – after crossing the Place de l'Estrapade with its trees, benches and a fountain – *rue de l'Estrapade.* These streets exude a tranquillity reminiscent of a provincial town. Thanks to the nearby Sorbonne University and some of the most elite schools in the country, this area is an important centre of intellectual life in the city.

❺ Panthéon

❻ Rue Mouffetard

❼ Place de la Contrescarpe

Stroll down rue Laromiguière, rue Amyot and rue Tournefort to rue Lohmond, and then turn left into the narrow Passage des Postes, which is noticeably livelier. A colourful market with many excellent fruit and veg stalls is situated at the lower end of the very old, yet always bustling ❻ Rue Mouffetard ➤ p. 42. The upper end of the "Mouff" definitely caters more to tourists. But the food stall Au p'tit Grec *(daily | tel. 06 50 24 69 34 | auptitgrec.com | €)* at no. 66 sells the best *galettes* (savoury crêpes, mostly made from buckwheat flour) in Paris. Eat your crêpe at the upper end of street on ❼ Place de la Contrescarpe, where street musicians play.

Café La Palette

The Grande Mosquée de Paris is an oriental oasis in the middle of the city

MUSEUMS, GARDENS AND A MOSQUE

From rue du Cardinal Lemoine (Ernest Hemingway once lived at no. 74), *walk down rue Rollin* with its old, crooked houses. *Go down the steps and across rue Monge* to the ❽ Arènes de Lutèce, a Roman amphi-theatre, on the left-hand side, which was first excavated in the 19th century. *Head right down rue Linné* (which turns into rue Geoffroy Saint-Hilaire) and go to the ❾ Jardin des Plantes ➤ p. 43, with its gardens, green-houses and the Muséum National d'Histoire Naturelle. *Continue along rue Buffon and rue Daubenton to the* Grande Mosquée de Paris. Delve into the Arab world at the end of your stroll with a mint tea and some sweet Middle Eastern pastries in the ❿ tea room at Mosquée de Paris *(daily | rue 39, Geoffroy St-Hilaire | 5th arr. | tel. 01 43 31 38 20 | la-mosquee.com/le-salon-de-the | €)* within the mosque complex.

❽ Arènes de Lutèce

❾ Jardin des Plantes

❿ tea room at Mosquée de Paris

❸ IN THE FOOTSTEPS OF THE ARTISTS OF MONTMARTRE

➤ Where Picasso and co. met
➤ Lose yourself in the little streets
➤ Paris as far as the eye can see from the Sacré-Cœur

⚐	Moulin Rouge	🏁	L'atelier Montmartre
→	2.4km	🚶	3 hours (40 minutes total walking time)

ⓘ The nearest Métro station to the start of the tour near Moulin Rouge: M 2 Blanche
The nearest Métro station to the last stop on the tour on rue Burg: M 12 Abbesses

THREE MILLS

The sex trade flourishes around the Métro station Blanche in ★ Montmartre, near the ❶ Moulin Rouge ➤ p. 114, which is still a favourite tourist attraction. Leave this slightly shabby area behind and *walk up the hill via rue Lépic*. Scenes from the cult film *Amélie* were shot at the Café des 2 Moulins at no. 15. Pop into the tiny, old-fashioned bakery across the street at no. 26, ❷ Les Petits Mitrons, whose window display is full of tasty looking tarts. Take in the village-like atmosphere *as you continue along rue Abesses, rue Durantin and up rue Tholozé. When you come to the top of rue Lépic,* enjoy the breathtaking view of the golden dome of Les Invalides ➤ p. 45, which shines above the sea of houses. On the corner of rue Lepic and rue Girardon is the Moulin de la Galette, an-other mill, moved here in 1924 from its original site nearby. A third mill had stood close to it and the garden between them had been a popular outdoor tavern or *guingette* in the 19th century, made famous by Auguste Renoir's painting *Bal du moulin de la Galette*. The restaurant ❸ Le Moulin de la Galette *(daily | 83 rue Lepic | tel. 01 46 06 84 77 |*

❶ Moulin Rouge

❷ Les Petits Mitrons

❸ Le Moulin de la Galette

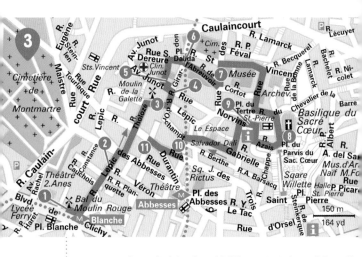

lemoulindelagalette.fr | €€) now sits in front of the mill – a great place to take your first break.

LITERATURE AND CHANSON

❹ Place Marcel Aymé

Afterwards, *head to* ❹ Place Marcel Aymé. Look out for the quizzical bronze figure emerging from a wall. The statue depicts the main character of the novella *Le Passemuraille (The Man Who Walked through Walls)* and is a tribute to the writer Marcel Aymé who once lived on this square. *Follow avenue Junot and then turn right at the end of rue Simon Dereure to get to the little park at* ❺ Square Suzanne Buisson. Sit down and stretch out your legs on one of the benches and admire the Statue des Saint Denis. St Denis is said to have walked the same route that you have been following up to now with his severed head in his hands. *Return to the entrance gate and then go up the steps to the right along a small idyllic path to* ❻ Place Dalida. The statue of the Egyptian-Italian singer (1933–87) looks up rue de l'Abreuvoir, which winds up the hill lined by small, crooked houses in a picture-perfect setting. *At the end of the street and down to the left on rue des Saules,* there is a surprising little ❼ vineyard. The grape harvest in October is celebrated with a festival every year, the Fête des Vendanges ➤ p. 121. A few yards further below, the famous cabaret Au Lapin Agile was once owned by

❺ Square Suzanne Buisson

❻ Place Dalida

❼ vineyard

the *chanson* singer Aristide Bruant, who is known to have supported many poor and unknown musicians.

CHURCH STEPS ABOVE THE ARTISTS' QUARTER
Rue Saint-Vincent will bring you closer to the back side of the gleaming white, almost Byzantine style basilica of ❽ Sacré-Cœur ➤ p. 63. Enjoy the view of Paris from the steps on the front side of the church. The narrow lanes around the church are filled with souvenir shops and tourists, and the ❾ Place du Tertre ➤ p. 63 is known for its many rather pushy portrait artists who will try to convince you to have your portrait drawn. *Walk down rue Norvins until you come to rue Gabrielle* (Pablo Picasso had his first studio in no. 49), *and then take rue Ravignan to the tree-lined Place Émile Goudeau*. In a studio within the house named ❿ Bateau-Lavoir, Picasso's famous cubist painting *Les Demoiselles d'Avignon* came to life. A bit further down, several lovely restaurants will tempt you to end this tour with a good meal. After that, pop into the bar ⓫ L'atelier Montmartre *(daily | 6 rue Burq | 18th arr. | tel. 01 42 51 32 27 | €)* – contemporary artists show their work here, and with a little luck, a happening will take place while you're there.

❽ Sacré-Cœur

❾ Place du Tertre

❿ Bateau-Lavoir

⓫ L'atelier Montmartre

Parisian vineyard in Montmartre

4 ISLANDS IN THE SEINE AND THE MARAIS

➤ Back to the Middle Ages
➤ Stop by the Notre-Dame to see the restoration
➤ Browse in the village of Saint-Paul

📍 Musée de Cluny   🏁 Musée Picasso

➡ 4km   🚶 6 hours (1 hour total walking time)

ℹ Costs: admission to Musée Picasso: 14 euros
The nearest Métro station to the start of the tour on Place Paul Painlevé: M 10 Cluny-La Sorbonne
The nearest Métro station to the last stop on the tour on rue de Thorigny: M 8 Chemin Vert

OLD CHURCHES, OLD TREES, OLD ISLANDS

❶ Musée de Cluny

❷ Saint-Séverin

The small park in the shadow of the Roman spas around the ❶ Musée de Cluny ➤ p. 41 is the perfect place to start off on the day's tour. A labyrinth of medieval streets begins *on the other side of boulevard Saint-Germain*, around the flamboyant Gothic-style church of ❷ Saint-Séverin. The distinguishing features of the church include its five-aisled nave and the double row of columns around the apse. The ribbed, vaulted ceiling resembles plant stalks, and there are colourful, modern stained-glass windows. The neighbourhood is full of inviting little cafés, such as La Fourmi Ailée ➤ p. 83, where you'll be tempted to linger, but also many restaurants that vie for tourist business.

❸ Saint-Julien-le-Pauvre

❹ Square Viviani

❺ Notre-Dame Cathedral

Just a short walk down rue Saint-Séverin will bring you to the small, stocky church of ❸ Saint-Julien-le-Pauvre, the oldest church in the city, dating back to the 12th century. From the adjacent park at ❹ Square Viviani, you can enjoy the view of the Seine as well as the boxes of Les Bouquinistes ➤ p. 92 and ❺ Notre-Dame Cathedral ➤ p. 39 in peace and quiet. At time of

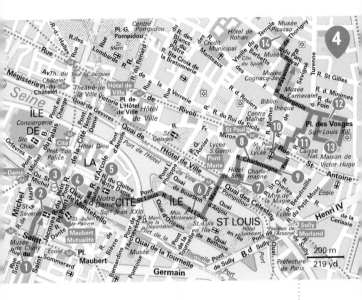

writing, the cathedral was still undergoing extensive renovations following the 2019 fire. A lovely garden brings life to the eastern side of the church. Look for the *little bridge that connects the Île de la Cité ➤ p. 30* with the Île Saint-Louis. Both islands, as the oldest parts of the city, are the real heart of Paris. Street artists almost always ply their trade on the strip connecting the two. Take some time to window shop on rue Saint-Louis-en-l'Île, with its lovely little shops, or head to ❻ Amorino *(daily 11am–11.55pm | 47 rue Saint-Louis-en-l'Île)* to sample the famous ice-cream flower that made the brand an international name.

❻ Amorino

ART AND HIDDEN TREAURES

The Pont Marie bridge will lead you directly into the Marais quarter. Directly to the right, at the corner of rue de l'Hôtel de Ville and rue du Figuier, the fortress-like late Gothic ❼ Hôtel de Sens, will surely catch your eye. This former second residence of the powerful bishops of the city of Sens now houses the art library Bibliothèque Forney, which regularly houses exhibitions *(paris.fr/lieux/bibliotheque-forney-18)*.

INSIDER TIP
Art in a library

❼ Hôtel de Sens

Look up and up and up again: the dome of the Baroque church of Saint-Paul

At the end of rue du Figuier, you will stumble upon rue Charlemagne and the charming little patio restaurant ⑧ Chez Mademoiselle (daily | rue Charlemagne 16 | 4th arr. | tel. 01 42 72 14 16 | chezmademoiselleparis.fr | €€). After a bite to eat, continue along rue Charlemagne, past the ruins of a tower and the old city walls dating back to the 13th century. Spend some time browsing through the courtyard labyrinth of ☂ ⑨ Village Saint-Paul ➤ p. 92, which is home to around 60 antiques dealers selling furniture, artworks, tableware, lamps and jewellery.

VISIT VICTOR HUGO AND PABLO PICASSO

Continue left up rue Saint-Paul to the Passage Saint-Paul, which leads through a side entrance into the three-storey Baroque church of ⑩ Saint-Paul with its large cupola. The traffic buzzes on rue Saint-Antoine in front of the main entrance. Walk a bit further towards the Bastille and turn left on rue Caron to get to the romantic ⑪ Place du Marché Sainte-Cathérine ➤ p. 37 with its

⑧ Chez Mademoiselle

⑨ Village Saint-Paul

⑩ Saint-Paul

⑪ Place du Marché Sainte-Cathérine

sycamore trees and cafés. Take a moment to catch your breath before *heading over rue de Turenne to the right onto the lively rue des Francs-Bourgeois,* which is lined by lovely aristocratic palaces. From here, it is just a short walk to the noble ⑫ Place des Vosges ➤ p. 37, one of the loveliest squares in the city. Take a walk around it, and, if you want, have a look at the former home (marked by the flag on the south-eastern corner of the square) of the French national poet at ⑬ Maison de Victor Hugo ➤ p. 36.

⑫ Place des Vosges

⑬ Maison de Victor Hugo

Cross back over the square to rue des Francs-Bourgeois, go right on rue Payenne, and turn via rue du Parc Royal into rue de Thorigny. The most extensive Picasso collection in the world awaits at the ⑭ Musée Picasso ➤ p. 36 in Hôtel Salé. End the day in style up on the museum's roof at the Café sur le toit *(Tue–Fri 10.30am–6pm, Sat/Sun 9.30am–6pm | €).*

⑭ Musée Picasso

This is where Victor Hugo started work on *Les Misérables*

❺ A WALK OF A DIFFERENT KIND BEHIND THE BASTILLE

➤ Stroll through old craftsmen's yards
➤ Boat show in the marina
➤ Climb into a green oasis

📍 Bastille Métro station

🏁 Jardin de Reuilly

→ 6.2km

🚶 5 hours (½ hour total walking time)

Métro lines to the starting point: M 1, 5, 8
Return to the centre or to Pachamama restaurant: M 8
Montgallet to Bastille
The Viaduc des Arts is open on Sundays.
The Passage Lhomme is only during the day on weekdays

WALK FROM COURTYARD TO COURTYARD

❶ Bastille Métro station

The ❶ Bastille Métro station marks the starting point for this tour to the east of the city centre. Nothing remains of the Bastille, the prison that was stormed in 1789 at the outbreak of the French Revolution. Today, the outline of the former structure is traced in stones different from the rest of the pavement on Place de la Bastille, where it intersects with Boulevard Henri IV. Go directly to the shining silver Opéra Bastille ➤ p. 54 and leave this huge, traffic-filled square in the *direction of rue du Faubourg Saint-Antoine.*

❷ Passage du Cheval Blanc

If you keep a lookout for hidden entrances, you will stumble upon some of the old craftsmen's workshops: *right at the start of rue de la Roquette* (Nr. 2), you will come upon the quiet ❷ Passage du Cheval Blanc, which is divided into courtyards named after the first six months of the year. *Turn right onto Cité Parchappe to return to rue du Faubourg Saint- Antoine,* which is lined by a string of idyllic courtyards.

A GOURMET TOUR

At no. 46, at the restaurant ❸ Pachamama *(Thu–Sat 8–10pm | tel. 01 55 78 84 75 | pachamama-paris.com | €€)*, where you should make reservations for the evening, you'll see architecture by Gustave Eiffel paired with South American flair. *Opposite, turn left onto rue de Charonne*, a lively shopping street. At no. 41, treat yourself to a *café crème* on the patio of the trendy ❹ Pause Café ➤ p. 84. Afterwards, cross through the lushly landscaped, picturesque ❺ Passage Lhomme *until it emerges onto avenue Ledru-Rollin.* Stop at no. 98 and select some chocolates from ❻ Chocolaterie Pause Détente *(closed Mon)* to eat as you walk.

Back on rue Faubourg Saint-Antoine, turn right into rue Croza-tier until you reach rue d'Aligre, which will take you directly to Place d'Aligre. At the 200-year-old, still very authentic market hall of ❼ Marché d'Aligre ➤ p. 101 you will find no end of delicious cheeses, hams, sausages and cold cuts. A good glass of wine and a few oysters at ❽ Le Baron Rouge ➤ p. 87 are just right for a little break.

INSIDER TIP
Feast like a god

❸ Pachamama

❹ Pause Café
❺ Passage Lhomme

❻ Chocolaterie Pause Détente

❼ Marché d'Aligre

❽ Le Baron Rouge

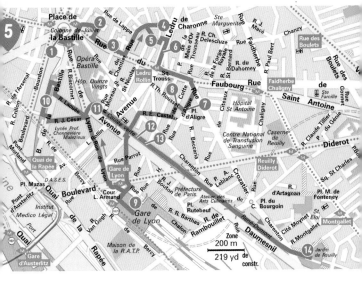

A STATION, A PORT AND A VIADUCT

With this fine taste lingering in your mouth, *follow rue Emilio Castelar and then rue Traversière to get to* ❾ Gare de Lyon, the loveliest railway station in the city and home to the legendary restaurant Le Train Bleu ➤ p. 79. Then take *rue de Lyon and rue Jules César* to the picture-perfect harbour ❿ Bassin de l'Arsenal. The port has an almost maritime flair thanks to the many yachts that put down anchor here. *Go back via rue Lacuée to avenue Daumnesnil,* which will bring you to this tour's major highlight: the ⓫ Coulée verte René-Dumont ➤ p. 55. These former train tracks, now surrounded by plenty of vegetation, lead 4.5km from the Bastille to the forest of Vincennes. For the first 1.5 km, the red-brick arches of the former railway viaduct have been glassed in to create studio space for all kinds of artisans and craftsmen.

DOZENS OF GREAT SHOPS

In the more than 50 studio shops within the ⓬ Viaduc des Arts ➤ p. 100, only the finest materials are used. Fashion designers, goldsmiths, picture restorers, glass-blowers and many shops selling art – as opposed to crafts – are housed in this innovative space. For something a bit different, check out the jewellery designer Tzuri Gueta (no. 1) who, among other things, creates silicon objects that resemble underwater plants. Interesting jewellery is also created at Cécile et Jeanne (no. 49). If you have deeper pockets, you can buy your own unique made-to-order handbag at Serge Amoruso (no. 37). If all this shopping has made you hungry, the best and most convenient place to go is the

⑬ Viaduc Café *at no 43 (daily | tel. 01 44 74 70 70 | leviaducdaumesnil | €).*

⑬ **Viaduc Café**

AN UPSTAIRS PARK

While products are made and sold in the shops below, you can walk along the viaduct's planted roof. *There are plenty of stairs that will take you up the 9 metres to the top.* Climb up and take the urban walking trail. Between the rose bushes, lavender and babbling water, you can appreciate the extraordinary view of the surrounding metropolitan area. As you *continue to the east*, you will come to the small park ⑭ Jardin de Reuilly, which is spanned by a footbridge and a favourite place among the locals in the neighbourhood during the summer. Take time to relax for a bit in the park before you head back to Place de la Bastille..

⑭ **Jardin de Reuilly**

Viaduc des Arts is an old railway viaduct that has been converted into elegant design studios

GOOD TO KNOW

HOLIDAY BASICS

ARRIVAL

PRE-TRIP INFORMATION

You'll find useful information on the French Tourist Board's *Explore France (france.fr)* website, and you can book accommodaton and activities with *Office du Tourisme et des Congrès de Paris (parisinfo.com)*

GETTING THERE

You can travel between London and Paris by coach for as little as £12 one way. Check out the National Express connections between London and Paris at nationalexpress.com.

The Eurostar from London arrives at the Gare du Nord. The railway station has a connection to the Métro network and RER. These tickets can be bought on the restaurant coaches of the trains. If you book early enough, you can travel from London to Paris return on Eurostar from 88 euros.

Approaching Paris by car, motorways all lead to the chaotic ring road Boulevard Périphérique (Périph for short) with 38 *"portes"* where you can enter and exit. The motorways are toll-based, with a speed limit of 130 kmh.

Due to stiff competition, you can often get a cheap flight to Paris by booking in advance, and even bargains can be found at short notice. Return flights are often available through *Easyjet* from 99 euros. Compare airfares on the Internet under *skyscanner.net*. Scheduled flights out of the UK land either at *Roissy-Charles-de-Gaulle (CDG)* airport north of Paris, or at *Orly (ORY)* to the south of the city.

You can get to and from the airport with public transport provided by RATP *(ratp.fr)*: It's fast and reliable, as long as there isn't a strike or an accident slowing things down. The suburban

Bustling street life in the Latin quarter

train line RER B travels from CDG via Paris to Antony every few minutes; from Antony, the Orlyval light railway runs to Orly Airport. *CDG–Paris: runs from shortly before 5am until just before midnight | travel time: 30–40 mins | 10.30 euros. ORY–Paris: 6am–11pm | travel time: 40 mins | 9.30 euros (RER plus Orlyval).*

The Roissy and Orly buses travel directly to Paris; the trip can take quite a bit longer if there's traffic. *CDG–Opéra: 6am–12.30am (runs from 5.15am in the opposite direction) every 15–20 mins | travel time: 60–75 mins | 13.70 euros. ORY–RER and Métro station Denfert-Rochereau: 6am–12.30 am (runs from 5.35am–midnight in the opposite direction) every 8–15 mins | travel time: approx. 30/40 mins | 9.50 euros.* WiFi on board.

The bus lines 350 (Gare de l'Est) and 351 (Nation) also run from Paris

to CDG Airport, as do the night bus lines N140 and N143. Bus line 183 (Porte de Choisy), tram line 7 and night buses N22, N31, N131 and N144 run to ORY. They're a bit cheaper, but they take longer because they make numerous stops.

Taxi: A ride downtown costs 53–58 euros from CDG and 32–37 euros from ORY.

GETTING AROUND

PUBLIC TRANSPORT

If you're in a hurry, it's best to take the Métro or the underground urban area RER railway. If you're changing trains and carrying heavy luggage, note that many stations have long passageways and flights of stairs.

RESPONSIBLE TRAVEL

It doesn't take a lot to be environmentally friendly while travelling. Don't just think about your carbon footprint while flying to and from your holiday destination but also about how you can protect nature and culture abroad. As a tourist it is especially important to respect nature, look out for local products, cycle instead of drive, save water and much more. If you would like to find out more about eco-tourism please visit: *ecotourism.org*

If you have time and want to see something of the city, buses and trams are perfect. This is especially the case for bus no. 73 (Arc de Triomphe, Champs-Elysées, Place de la Concorde, Musée d'Orsay) and no. 21 (Opéra Garnier, Palais Royal, Louvre, Île de la Cité, St-Michel, Jardin du Luxembourg, rue Mouffetard). ☛ This way, a city tour bus will only cost you 1.90 euros!

INSIDER TIP
See Paris on the cheap

Métro and RER operate 5.30am–1.15am, and an hour longer on Friday, Saturday and before holidays. Buses, depending on the line, start later in the morning and stop their service earlier in the evening. Night buses *(noctilien)* run between 12.30am and 5.30am. Timetables for all Métro, RER, tram and bus lines are available at all stations and at *ratp.fr* or the *Bonjour RATP* app.

Single tickets *ticket t+* are valid within the city limits for the Métro, RER, tram and buses. They are valid for 1.5 hours on the Métro, RER, bus or tram, with as many transfers as you wish. Be aware that changing from Métro/RER to a bus or tram will cost you a further single ticket.

Paper blocks of ten are no longer sold, but instead rechargeable plastic cards called Navigo Easy are available. These can be purchased for 2 euros at tobacco shops marked with the ticket logo, and in all Métro and RER stations. Paper tickets are available directly from bus drivers (10 cents surcharge, valid only on the same bus).

Unfortunately, SMS bus tickets only work with a French mobile phone contract, and the *Bonjour RATP* app currently only offers ticket sales for some mobile phone models. If yours isn't one of them, you can use the app to load tickets onto your Navigo Easy card. It is more economical to purchase a book of 10 tickets *(carnet)* for 14.90 euros. 👫 Children up to four years of age travel for free, with a special rate for children between four and 10.

The day card *Carte Mobilis* (paper ticket) or *Forfait Navigo Jour* (Navigo Easy) for Paris costs 7.50 euros, or 17.80 euros for all zones. The *Paris Visite* ticket costs 12 euros per day for Paris and the adjacent suburbs and 38.35 euros for all zones. It offers additional discounts for several attractions.

The *Paris Navigo Decouverte* (22.80 euros/week, 75.20 euros/month, plus 5 euros for the ticket and a passport photo) is ideal for a longer Paris stay. It allows you to travel as often as you wish in all zones all week. However, you can only purchase these tickets at the beginning of the week/month.

CYCLING

If you want to explore Paris by bicycle, take a *Vélib' (velibmetropole.fr)*. Now, you can also rent e-bikes (in blue) at the company's approximately 1,400 docking stations throughout the city. If you choose one of the green Vélib' models, though, you'll have to work the pedals yourself.

For a day ticket, you'll pay a base price of 5 euros. The first half hour on a normal bicycle is free; each half hour after that costs 1 euro. For an e-bike, the first 45 minutes cost 2 euros, and each half hour after that costs 2 euros. You'll find a Vélib' station every 300 metres or so. By the way, if the seat of a parked bicycle is turned backwards, it means that the last rider discovered the bicycle doesn't work properly. The Vélib' app is really practical: it shows you where the closest station is located and how many bicycles are currently available there.

Private providers have been competing with Vélib' since 2017 and manage without a docking station at all. The market is highly competitive. While many of the early start-ups have already withdrawn, others are trying their luck, with more and more e-bikes on offer. You can locate, unlock and pay for the bikes via the respective apps.

There are little signs on many traffic lights to indicate to cyclists that they can turn right or keep going straight when the light turns red.

DRIVING

A car really isn't necessary in Paris, but if you do need one, many Parisians now turn to car sharing *(ubeeqo.com, paris.communauto.com)* or borrow a car from a private individual *(getaround.com)*.

Driving in Paris is no fun at all: loads of traffic, expensive car parks that are always full, an eternal search for a free spot, wheel clamps and tow trucks for parking offenders. If you can't do without a car, make sure your accommodation offers parking, or reserve a space in a car park using, for example, *parkingsdeparis.com/EN*.

Keep in mind: A Crit'Air sticker is compulsory in Paris. This emissions sticker is available in six different versions. On weekdays from 8am to 8pm, vehicles with high emissions are not permitted on the roads, with more and more cars to be impacted in the coming years (see p. 22/23). The sticker must be placed in a visible location on the inside of the vehicle's windscreen, or the driver will face a fine of 68 euros. The sticker costs 4.80 euros and can be ordered online from the French environmental ministry's website: *certificat-air.gouv.fr*.

E-MOPEDS

Several thousand electric mopeds are available across the city. *Cityscoot (cityscoot.eu)* charges between 28 and 39 cents per minute, and the pioneering provider has since been joined by other rental companies like *Cooltra (cooltra.com)* and *Yego (landing. rideyego.com/paris)*.

E-SCOOTERS

Electric scooters are a nifty option for covering short distances within the city centre. As the American trend started to catch on in Europe, several providers like *Lime (li.me)* were quick to install their e-scooters along the Seine. Find and unlock the scooters via the respective app. It costs around 1 euro basic fee plus 25 cents/minute.

TAXI

Taxis charge a maximum base fee of 4.18 euros and cost around 1.50 euros per km (depending on the time of travel) with a minimum fare of 7.30 euros. There are additional costs for reservations, waiting times and parties of more than four passengers, but not for luggage. The only fixed prices are for trips to the airport (see p. 148).

Taxi G7: tel. 01 47 39 47 39 | g7.fr is an app with integrated payment function.

VTC (CAR WITH DRIVER)

You can book and pay for trips with a VTC (*Voiture de Tourisme avec Chauffeur)* via the corresponding app: *Uber (uber.com), leCab (tel. 08 92 56 25 00 (*) | lecab.fr), Marcel (tel. 01 70 95 14 15 | marcel.cab)*. Great deals for early bookers!

EMERGENCIES

BRITISH EMBASSY

35 rue du Faubourg St Honoré | 75383 Paris Cedex 08 | tel. 01 44 51 31 00 | gov.uk/government/world/france

EMBASSY OF THE UNITED STATES

2 avenue Gabriel | 75008 Paris Cedex 08 | tel. 01 43 12 22 22 | usembassy. gov/france

EMBASSY OF CANADA

130 rue du Faubourg St Honoré | 75008 Paris | tel. 01 44 43 29 00 | canadainternational.gc.ca/france/offices-bureaux/contact.aspx?lang=eng

EMERGENCY NUMBERS

Ambulance (Samu): *15*
Police: *17*
Fire department, First Aid: *18*
Medical emergencies (SOS Médecins): *01 47 07 77 77*
Dental emergencies: *01 43 37 51 00*

HEALTH

UK and US citizens should buy travel insurance that will cover any medical expenses. EU citizens should carry the EHIC card, which gives them the right to access the French healthcare system. You will have to pay first and reclaim the expenses later.

Chemists *(pharmacies)* are denoted by a green cross and are generally open until 8pm Monday–Saturday, or even later. Pharmacies open at night and on the weekend can be found at *monopharmacien-idf.fr.*

LOST PROPERTY OFFICE

The traditional lost property office has been replaced by an online service. Report any lost property at *ppbot.fr.*

ESSENTIALS

CITY TOURS

Of course, Paris has sightseeing buses: *bigbustours.com/paris* or *paris.open tour.com*, but that's not all.

4 roues sous 1 parapluie (Four Wheels Under One Umbrella) is a classic. Travel from tourist attraction to tourist attraction in a Citroën 2CV. The chauffeurs have loads of great tips up their sleeves *(tours from 20 euros/person | tel. 01 58 59 27 82 | 4roues-sous-1parapluie.com/fr).*

Growing numbers of tour guides are using Paris's improved cycle infrastructure to offer tours. Many English tours are available from companies like *Paris Bike Tour (tours from 39 euros | 13 rue Brantôme | tel. 01 42 74 22 14 | parisbiketour.net | 3rd arr. | M 11 Rambuteau).*

CUSTOMS

UK citizens can bring up to 42 litres of beer, 18 litres of wine and 4 litres of spirits, plus 200 cigarettes, back from France for personal use.

EVENT TIPS

L'Officiel du Spectacle (1.80 euros) provide an overview of what's on in Paris. Published every Wednesday, also available as an app *(offi.fr).*

INTERNET ACCESS & WIFI

Around 300 public squares, parks, and buildings such as libraries and the Centre Pompidou offer l free WiFi. An increasing number of cafés, bars, restaurants, as well as hotels and youth hostels, also provide *wifi gratuit*. Some Métro and RER stations are equipped with internet stations with free access, but so far only at the Point Connect charging points themselves (see p. 152). In the metro itself, you'll have to go without for long stretches underground.

HOW MUCH IS IT?

Coffee	2.50 euros for an espresso
Snack	3-8 euros for a ham sandwich
Wine	4.50–20 euros for a glass of table wine
Métro	1.90 euros for a single ticket
Souvenir	18.50 euros for 6 macarons from Ladurée
Taxi	9 euros for a short trip of around 4km

PHONES

All Paris numbers (with the exception of special internet landline numbers beginning with 09) begin with 01. Mobile numbers start with 06 or 07, with some special numbers beginning with 08. The country code for the UK is +44, for the USA +1, followed by the area code without a zero. When calling from overseas, +33 must be dialled for Paris phone numbers (leaving out the zero).

The French word for mobile phone is *portable*. You can charge your mobile at the new bus stops in Paris with a USB cable, or at "Point Connect" WiFi hotspots in many metro stations.

POST

After four years of renovations, the historic main office has reopened (*Mon–Sat 8am–midnight, Sun 10am–midnight | 52 rue du Louvre | 1st arr. | M 4 Les Halles | laposte.fr*). The cost of sending postcards and letters up to 20 grams worldwide is 1.65 euros.

PUBLIC HOLIDAYS

1 January	New Year's Day
March/April	Easter Monday
1 May	Labour Day
8 May	Victory Day
mid-May	Ascension Day
14 July	Bastille Day
15 Aug	Assumption of Mary
1 Nov	All Saints' Day
11 Nov	Armistice Day
25 Dec	Christmas

SEINE EXCURSIONS

Numerous tourist boats are waiting to take you past the Eiffel Tower, Louvre and Notre-Dame. You can choose between sightseeing and restaurant trips. The *bateaux mouches (all year round, as often as every 30mins in high season | departure: Port de la Conférence, Pont de l'Alma | M 9 Alma-Marceau | trip length: 70 mins | 15 euros, with lunch 69 euros, with dinner from 79 euros | bateaux-mouches.fr*) are legendary.

Or take a *Batobus (batobus.com)*. These ferries stop at nine spots, where you can embark and disembark as you please. Frequency and departure times vary depending according to the season. *Daily 10am–7pm (at least every 30 mins) | day ticket 19 euros, 17 euros online.*

🎭 *Marcel le Canard (canardsdeparis.com)* is the first French amphibious bus from *Les Canards de Paris (Ducks of Paris)*. Just like a duck, Marcel is happy on land and in the water but can't fly! *In high season, several departures daily from Place Jacques Rueff near the Eiffel Tower | duration 1 hr 45 mins, of which approx. 20–25 mins are spent on the Seine | 38 euros (children 2–11 years 22 euros).*

TICKET SALES

Visit one of the eleven Paris branches of *Fnac*, or order at fnacspectacles.com.

👉 Reduced-price theatre and concert tickets are available at *billetreduc.com* in the *Réductions* section. And it doesn't get better than this: you can even download free tickets for selected events under *"Invitations"*.

TOURIST INFORMATION

Main office: *Hôtel de Ville (daily 10am–6pm, July/Aug 9.30am–6.30pm | 29 rue de Rivoli | 4th arr. | M 1, 11 Hôtel de Ville)*.

Gare du Nord (daily 9am–5pm | 18 rue de Dunkerque | 10th arr. | M 4, 5 Gare du Nord | RER B, D Gare du Nord).

Carrousel du Louvre (Wed–Mon 10am–8pm, Tue 11am–8pm | 99 rue de Rivoli | 1st arr. | M 1, 7 Palais Royal-Musée du Louvre).

Cycling tour along the River Seine

WEATHER IN PARIS

High season
Low season

	JAN	FEB	MARCH	APRIL	MAY	JUNE	JULY	AUG	SEPT	OCT	NOV	DEC
Daytime temperature	1°	3°	8°	14°	20°	23°	25°	24°	21°	16°	10°	7°
Night-time temperature	1°	1°	4°	6°	10°	13°	15°	14°	12°	8°	5°	2°
Sunshine hours/day	2	3	5	7	7	7	7	7	6	4	2	2
Rainy days/month	12	10	8	9	9	9	9	9	9	8	10	10

☀ Sunshine hours/day   🌧 Rainy days/month

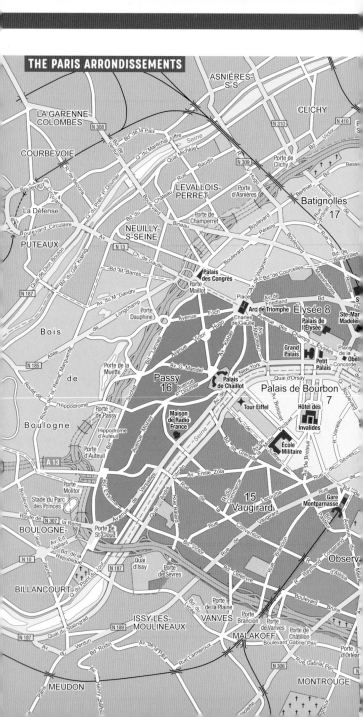

THE PARIS ARRONDISSEMENTS

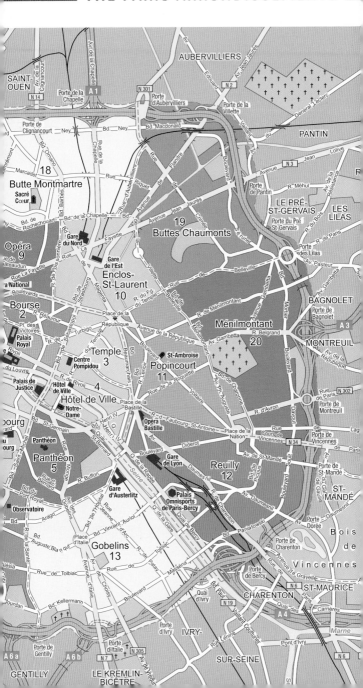

WORDS & PHRASES
IN FRENCH

SMALL TALK

yes/no/perhaps	oui/non/peut-être
please	s'il vous plaît
thank you	merci
Good morning!/Good evening!/Goodnight!	Bonjour!/Bonsoir!/Bonne nuit!
Hello!/Goodbye!	Salut!/Au revoir!
My name is…	Je m'appelle …
I am from…	Je suis de …
Excuse me!	Pardon!
How?	Comment?
I (don't) like that.	Ça (ne) me plaît (pas).
I would like…	Je voudrais …
Do you have… ?	Avez-vous?

SYMBOLS

EATING & DRINKING

The menu, please.	La carte, s'il vous plaît.
Please may I have… ?	Puis-je avoir … s'il vous plaît?
bottle/carafe/glass	bouteille/carafe/verre
knife/fork/spoon	couteau/fourchette/cuillère
salt/pepper/sugar	sel/poivre/sucre
vinegar/oil	vinaigre/huile
milk/cream/lemon	lait/crème/citron
with/without ice/gas	avec/sans glaçons/gaz
vegetarian	végétarien(ne)
I would like to pay, please.	Je voudrais payer, s'il vous plaît.

MISCELLANEOUS

Where is…?/Where are…?	Où est …?/Où sont …?
What time is it?	Quelle heure est-il?
today/tomorrow/yesterday	aujourd'hui/demain/hier
How much is…?	Combien coûte …?
Help!/Careful!	Au secours!/Attention!
fever/pains	fièvre/douleurs
chemist/pharmacy	pharmacie/droguerie
open/closed	ouvert/fermé
good/bad	bon/mauvais
left/right/straight ahead	à gauche/à droite/tout droit
broken/garage	panne/garage
timetable/ticket	horaire/billet
0/1/2/3/4/5/6/7/8/9/10/100/1000	zéro/un, une/deux/trois/quatre/cinq/six/sept/huit/neuf/dix/cent/mille

HOLIDAY VIBES
FOR RELAXATION & CHILLING

FOR BOOKWORMS & FILM BUFFS

📖 750 YEARS IN PARIS

This book tells the story of Paris based on a single house, and without a single word. Parisian illustrator Vincent Mahé drew the same house 60 times, illustrating how it changed over the course of history, from 1265 to the attack on *Charlie Hebdo* in 2015.

📖 PARIS 2119

In this dark vision from comic authors Zep and Bertail, people no longer travel to Paris by train or plane but beam themselves to the Seine by transponder.

🎥 LOST IN PARIS

This is a poetic comedy: the story of a Canadian librarian who travels to Paris looking for her elderly aunt and meets a homeless Parisian man. The 2017 film by and starring Fiona Gordon shows both the beautiful and the dark sides of the city of lights.

🎥 MISSION IMPOSSIBLE – FALLOUT

Secret agent Ethan Hunt (Tom Cruise) flies around the Eiffel Tower, races around the Arc de Triomphe, parachutes onto the Grand Palais and navigates underground canals (2018).

PLAYLIST ON SHUFFLE

0:58

II CAMILLE – PARIS
While determined to escape Paris and its dirty pavements, the singer somehow returns time and again

▶ SETH GUEKO, NEKFEU & OXMO PUCCINO – TITI PARISIEN
A tribute to Paris from the three French rappers, recorded after the attacks on 13 November 2015

▶ RYADH – JE T'AIME
There are a thousand reasons to hate Paris, but then there are a thousand reasons to love it too

▶ JACQUES DUTRONC – PARIS S'ÉVEILLE
Early-morning Paris when lovers are exhausted and strippers are fully dressed again

▶ JOE DASSIN – LES CHAMPS-ÉLYSÉES
An ode to the famous boulevard

Your holiday soundtrack can be found on **Spotify** under **MARCO POLO Paris**

Or scan this code with the Spotify app

ONLINE

MYLITTLEPARIS.COM
Lifestyle tips – including restaurants, beauty and fashion – as well as inside information on special sales and more

PARIS JE T'AIME
Official website of the Paris Tourist office, packed with information on districts and sights, Paris for families or lovers, plus sport, shopping and restaurants, and much more *(paris jetaime.com)*

QUEFAIRE.PARIS
A shared calendar managed by the city of Paris; private individuals as well as club and event location managers can announce events here. *(paris.fr/quefaire)*

SPOTTEDBYLOCALS.COM/PARIS
Parisians and newcomers post articles here about their favourite spots in the city – cool and casual. Also available as an app for a few euros

TRAVEL PURSUIT

THE MARCO POLO HOLIDAY QUIZ

Do you know what makes Paris tick? Test your knowledge of the idiosyncrasies and eccentricities of the city and its people. You'll find the answers at the foot of the page, with more detailed explanations on pages 20 to 25.

❶ How many Métro stations are there in Paris?
a) Around 700
b) Over 300
c) Just under 500

❷ What is the "Plan Vigipirate"?
a) Security measures to prevent terrorist attacks
b) A programme to boost the local economy
c) A series of measures to make the city greener

❸ Who said Berlin could never compete with Paris?
a) Napoleon Bonaparte
b) Frederick the Great
c) The Sun King Louis XIV

❹ When does the hot air balloon in Parc André Citroën change colour to red?
a) For Valentine's Day
b) When there is a terrorist alert
c) When air pollution levels are high

❺ What do you get if you order a *carafe d'eau*?
a) Sparkling water
b) Still bottled water
c) Tap water

❻ When was the first public film screening in Paris?
a) 1859
b) 1895
c) 1903

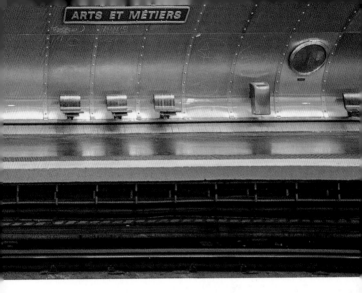

The gleaming copper Arts et Métiers metro station was inspired by Jules Verne's *Nautilus*

❼ What does the city's motto: "Fluctuat nec mergitur" mean?
a) She is tossed by the waves but doesn't sink
b) Refugees welcome
c) The city ebbs and flows

❽ When will all vehicles with internal combustion engines be banned from the city?
a) 2030
b) 2035
c) 2040

❾ Why do Parisians love a picnic so much?
a) It's tricky to find a table without a reservation
b) Prices in restaurants and bars are pretty steep
c) They don't! A Parisian would never sit on the ground!

❿ The Champs-Élysées …
a) … are completely free of traffic and have been since 2019
b) … are only an option for cars with special permission
c) … are car-free for one Sunday each month

⓫ Before 2024, when were the Olympic Games last held in Paris?
a) 1984
b) 1900
c) 1924

⓬ What does Paris owe to British patron Richard Wallace?
a) Street lamps
b) Drinking fountains
c) Dog toilets

INDEX

INDEX & CREDITS

WE WANT TO HEAR FROM YOU!

Did you have a great holiday? Is there something on your mind? Whatever it is, let us know! Whether you want to praise the guide, alert us to errors or give us a personal tip – MARCO POLO would be pleased to hear from you.

We do everything we can to provide the very latest information for your trip. Nevertheless, despite all of our authors' thorough research, errors can creep in. MARCO POLO does not accept any liability for this.

Please contact us by email:

sales@heartwoodpublishing.co.uk

MARCO POLO AUTHOR
FELICITAS SCHWARZ GRAMMON

Felicitas had only planned on studying at the Sorbonne for a year, but that one year quickly evolved into something much longer – 15, in fact! The journalist finally left the city for Alsace shortly before the Covid-19 pandemic, but whenever she returns and crosses one of the many bridges over the Seine, she is reminded once again why she fell for Paris.

DOS & DON'TS

HOW TO AVOID SLIP-UPS & BLUNDERS

DON'T STAND ON THE LEFT SIDE OF AN ESCALATOR
There's an unwritten rule when it comes to Paris escalators: if you stand on the left – the fast lane – in a Métro station or department store, expect Parisians to give you a reproachful look and to hear annoyed shouts of "pardon!". If you've got time to spare, stick to the right.

DON'T SEAT YOURSELF AT A RESTAURANT
In a restaurant, don't make a beeline for the nearest table. In Paris it is customary to wait for a waiter to show you to your table. However, you may be able to change tables if the one initially chosen is not to your liking.

DON'T WAIT FOR THE CARS TO STOP AT A ZEBRA CROSSING
Because you might be waiting a while! In theory, drivers are supposed to stop, but in Parisian practice, most drivers are only prepared to do so if you practically throw yourself at their bonnet. Your best bet is to follow a local who will know exactly when and how to cross the street in one piece!

DON'T STAY SEATED ON THE MÉTRO'S FOLDING SEATS
There are folding seats right next to the doors of the train on many Métro lines. You can use them as long as the Métro is relatively empty, but follow experienced Métro riders when they stand up to make room for newly boarded passengers, or you might find a handbag or rucksack in your face.

DON'T THROW YOUR CIGARETTE BUTTS IN THE ROAD
It'll cost you! Parisian street sweepers collected 350 tons of cigarette butts in a year. That figure is now being converted into cash! 135 euros per butt.